Mitchell Symons was born in London and educated at Mill Hill School and the LSE, where he studied law. Since leaving BBC TV, where he was a researcher and then a director, he has worked as a writer, broadcaster and journalist. He was a principal writer of early editions of the board game Trivial Pursuit and has devised many television formats. He is also the author of more than thirty books, and currently writes a weekly column for the Sunday Express. *Why Eating Bogeys Is Good for You* won the Blue Peter Best Book with Facts Award in 2010 and he repeated this success with *Do Igloos Have Loos?* in 2011.

www.**grossbooks**.co.uk

How much yucky stuff do you know?

Collect all these gross fact books
by Mitchell Symons!

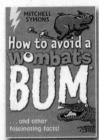

Available now!

Why don't you smell when you're sleeping?

Mitchell Symons

DOUBLEDAY

WHY DON'T YOU SMELL WHEN YOU'RE SLEEPING?
A DOUBLEDAY BOOK 978 1 085 753098 1
Published in Great Britain by Doubleday, an imprint of
Random House Children's Publishers UK
A Random House Group Company

This edition published 2014

1 3 5 7 9 10 8 6 4 2

Copyright © Mitchell Symons, 2014
Illustrations copyright © Nigel Baines, 2014

The Random House Group Limited supports the Forest Stewardship
Council (FSC®), the leading international forest certification organization.
Our books carrying the FSC label are printed on FSC®-certified paper.
FSC is the only forest certification scheme endorsed by the leading
environmental organizations, including Greenpeace.
Our paper procurement policy can be found at
www.randomhouse.co.uk/environment.

MIX
Paper from
responsible sources
FSC
www.fsc.org   FSC® C016897

Set in Optima

RANDOM HOUSE CHILDREN'S PUBLISHERS UK
61–63 Uxbridge Road, London W5 5SA

www.randomhousechildrens.co.uk

Addresses for companies within The Random House Group Limited
can be found at: www.randomhouse.co.uk/offices.htm
THE RANDOM HOUSE GROUP Limited Reg. No. 954009

A CIP catalogue record for this book is available from the British Library.

Printed and bound in Great Britain by Clays Ltd, St Ives plc

To YOU, the returning reader.
Thanks for your loyalty.
To YOU, the new reader.
Thanks for giving me a chance.

Introduction

OK, regular readers (and a big welcome back to you!) will have got the drill by now and can start gorging themselves on all the new trivia I've found for you.

Newcomers (and a big hello to you!) should start here.

This is the thirteenth book in a series that started with *How To Avoid A Wombat's Bum*. But, within those eleven books, it's also the fourth pure trivia book. The other three being *How To Avoid A Wombat's Bum, How Much Poo Does An Elephant Do?* and *Why Does Ear Wax Taste So Gross?*

I've been collecting great trivia for over 30 years now and I still get a big buzz from finding a wonderful fact.

To write this book, I used my large library of reference books as well as the internet (although I tried to use this to check facts rather than, as is so tempting, as a tool of first resort).

Now for some important acknowledgements because without these people, this book couldn't have been written at all: (in alphabetical order): my fantastic editor Lauren Buckland, my wife and chief researcher Penny Chorlton, my lovely publisher Annie Eaton, and Nigel Baines.

In addition, I'd also like to thank the following people for their help, contributions and/or support: Gilly Adams, Luigi Bonomi, Paul Donnelley, Jonathan Fingerhut, Jenny Garrison, Philip Garrison, William Mulcahy, Nicholas Ridge, Charlie Symons, Jack Symons, Louise Symons, David Thomas and Martin Townsend, Harriet Venn, Clair Woodward and Rob Woolley.

If I've missed anyone out, then please know that – as with any mistakes in the book – it is, as I always say, entirely down to my own stupidity.

Mitchell Symons

P.S. How quickly can you find the fact that relates to the title of the book?

Firsts

The first astronauts to go to the moon trained in Iceland because the terrain was reckoned to be similar to the moon's surface.

The first pull-top can was invented by Ermal Cleon Fraze in 1959, after he had to resort to using his car bumper to open a can of drink.

The first commercial vacuum cleaner was so large it was mounted on a wagon. People threw parties in their homes so guests could watch the new device do its job.

The first TV remote control – named Lazy Bones – was sold by Zenith in the US in 1950. It was connected to the set by a wire.

The first person killed in a car accident was Londoner Bridget Driscoll, who was run over in 1896 by a car travelling at four miles per hour.

Bugs Bunny was the first cartoon character to be pictured on a US postage stamp.

Leonardo da Vinci was the first person to record that the number of rings in the cross section of a tree trunk revealed its age. He also discovered that the width

between the rings indicated the annual rainfall.

The first alarm clock could only ring at four a.m. I don't think that would have sold very well!

The first electric razor was invented by Jacob Schick during the First World War, while he was in the US Army and stationed at an Alaskan army base. Tired of breaking the layer of ice that formed in the washbasin so that he could shave, he developed an electric razor which he patented in 1923. In 1931 his razor went on sale to the public (for $25), and he had sold nearly two million by 1937.

The first Briton to be killed in a flying accident was Charles Rolls (of Rolls-Royce fame).

The first bagpipe was made from the liver of a dead sheep.

The first televised Wimbledon tennis match was in 1937.

The Olympic Games were filmed for the first time in 1936 in Berlin. However, the footage was not shown on home televisions, but on large screens around the city.

The first Olympic Games to be covered for a worldwide TV audience were the Rome Olympics of 1960.

The butterfly swimming event was first held at the 1956 Olympics. In fact, the

event had been added to the Games because some swimmers were exploiting a loophole to swim butterfly in the breaststroke race!

France can boast the world's first department store: Le Bon Marché, which opened in Paris in 1838.

Ties (as in neckties) were first worn at the time of the Thirty Years War (1618 – 48) when the traditional small, knotted neckerchiefs worn by Croatian mercenaries fighting for the French were adopted as ties by Parisians.

While we're in Croatia . . . the Statute of Korcula – which was drafted in the Croatian town of the same name in 1214 and signed in 1265 – was the first European Act to prohibit trading in slaves. Korcula is also claimed as a possible birthplace of the explorer Marco Polo.

The world's first university was established in Takshila, India (now in Pakistan), in 700

BC. Over 10,500 students from all over the world studied more than 60 subjects, including algebra, trigonometry and calculus, which were all first studied in India.

Belgium was the first country to issue electronic passports.

San Marino entered the Eurovision Song Contest for the first time in 2008.

Africa's first republic, Liberia, was founded in 1822 thanks to the efforts of the American Colonization Society, which decided to settle freed American slaves in West Africa. Liberia, which means 'land of the free', became home to (as they were known) Americo-Liberians, who established a settlement in Monrovia (named after US President James Monroe).

In 1993 the Netherlands became the first country to allow euthanasia (mercy-killing for the terminally ill) under certain strict conditions.

Singapore is home to the world's first night zoo: the Night Safari.

The Indian mathematician Aryabhatta first came up with the mathematical concept of zero at the end of the fifth century.

Abba's *Waterloo* was the first Eurovision Song Contest entry to reach the US Top Ten.

The first internet hoax to reach a mass audience was the 1994 claim that Microsoft had bought the Catholic Church.

A Japanese surgeon named Hanaoka Seish performed the world's first operation under general anaesthesia in 1804.

An American inventor named William Bullock patented the first continuous-roll printing press (also known as a web rotary printing press) in 1863, which went on to revolutionize the printing industry. Four years later, his invention killed him when his leg got caught in the machine and he developed gangrene.

The world's first oil wells were drilled in China in the fourth century AD.

Onlys

There are only four clubs in the English Football League with names that start and end with the same letter: Liverpool,

Charlton Athletic, Northampton Town and Aston Villa.

Alaska is the only US state that can be typed on a single row of a keyboard (the middle row!).

David Duchovny is the only actor to win a Golden Globe for both Drama and Comedy.

The only mammal species in which the female is normally taller than the male is a type of antelope called an okapi.

Henry VII was the only English king to be crowned on a field of battle.

There are only eight different surnames on the island of Tristan da Cunha. They are: Glass, Green, Hagan, Lavarello, Patterson, Repetto, Rogers and Swain.

New Hampshire is the only US state where adults don't have to wear seat belts in cars.

Three babies have been born on the London Underground. The first was called Thelma

Ursula Beatrice Eleanor. She was born in 1924 on a Bakerloo line train at Elephant & Castle. Check out her initials!

***The Comedy of Errors* is the only Shakespeare play that doesn't have a song in it.**

Bhutan is the only country that officially measures its nation's level of happiness.

Until 1896, India was the world's only source of diamonds.

Guyana is the only English-speaking country in South America.

Saudi Arabia is the only country where women aren't allowed to drive.

The United States and the Philippines are the only countries that allow bounty hunting.

Sailing is the only sport that has a triangular course.

In 1894 Earl Rosebery became the only Prime Minister to own a Derby winner.

An Austrian man named Adam Rainer (1899 – 1950) is the only man in recorded human history ever to have been both a dwarf and a giant. At the age of 21 he was just 3 foot, 10½ inches, but then he had growth spurts that saw him grow to an incredible 7 foot, 8 inches.

New Zealand is the only country that has every type of climate in the world.

Sir Ken Adam, the original production designer of the James Bond films, was the only German to fight for the RAF in the Second World War.

There are only two full-length Disney feature films in which both parents of the main characters are present and alive throughout the movie: *101 Dalmatians* and *Peter Pan*.

Harry Lee played his only Test cricket match in 1931 – some 15 years after being declared dead in the First World War.

Words

Thirteen per cent of the letters in any given book are 'e'.

Using only the right-hand side of a keyboard, the longest word that can be typed is 'johnny-jump-up', or, excluding hyphens, 'hypolimnion'.

Here is a six-word sequence in which each new word is formed by adding one letter to the beginning of the previous word:

hes *(plural of 'he', used as a noun to mean a male)*
shes *(plural of 'she')*
ashes
lashes
plashes *(plural of 'plash', a splashing sound)*
splashes

The word 'gorilla' comes from the Carthaginian language of Tunisia.

'Widow' is the only female word in the English language that is shorter than its corresponding male term (widower).

There are only two words in English that end in the letters 'shion' – 'cushion' and 'fashion'.

A kangaroo word is one that contains all the letters, in order, of another word that has the same meaning. Examples include

'masculine' (male), 'observe' (see) and 'inflammable' (flammable).

The three-syllable word 'hideous', with the change of a single letter, becomes a two-syllable word with no vowel sounds in common: 'hideout'.

There are only three English words that end in the letters 'cion'. These are 'coercion', 'scion', and 'suspicion'.

'Zzyzx', a place in California, and 'zyzzyx', a type of wasp, consist of only the last three letters of the alphabet.

For many years, the word 'set' had the longest entry in the *Oxford English Dictionary*, but it has now been overtaken by the word 'make'. 'Make' and 'set' are followed by 'run', 'take' and 'go' – in that order.

The word 'Iouea' (a genus of sea sponges), is the only word to contain all five vowels and no other letters.

The English-language alphabet originally had only 24 letters. The letters 'U' and 'J' are both more recent additions.

There are only two sequences of four letters in alphabetical order that can be found in English words: 'rstu' and 'mnop'. Examples of each are 'understudy' and 'gymnophobia'.

The word 'shampoo' comes from the Hindu word 'champo', meaning 'to massage'.

Faulconbridge, a town in the Blue Mountains of Australia, uses half the alphabet, including all five vowels, and doesn't use any individual letter twice.

Words that came to English via the Czech language include 'robot', 'pistol' and 'dollar'.

The ten-letter word 'soupspoons' consists entirely of letters from the second half of alphabet, as does the hyphenated 'topsy-turvy'.

'Asthma' and 'isthmi' are the only six-letter words that begin and end with a vowel, and have no other vowels in between.

Contranyms

A contranym is a single word that has

opposite meanings, for example:

'Sanction' can mean approve or punish.

'Clip' can mean to cut or to fasten (clip together).

'Cleave' can mean to split apart or to join together.

'Screen' can mean to shield or to present.

'Bound' can mean to be going (to be bound for London) or to be tied up (unable to move).

'Left' can mean remaining or to have gone.

Palindromes

A palindrome is a word or sentence that reads the same backwards or forwards – like 'Madam, I'm Adam'.

Here are some more:

A Santa deified at NASA

A coup d'état saved devastated Puoca

A new order began, a more Roman age bred Rowena

Denim axes examined

Dennis and Edna sinned

Feeble Tom's motel beef

Lisa Bonet ate no basil

Fascinating facts

Prince Charles and Prince William never travel on the same aeroplane as a precaution against both of them being involved in a crash.

One per cent of Greenland's population lives in a single apartment building.

Oprah Winfrey makes all her employees sign lifelong confidentiality agreements.

In 1930 the Mars family launched their

They named it Snickers after their favourite
horse.

**The longest recorded Monopoly game took
1,680 hours – more than 70 days.**

Lake Baikal in Siberia contains 20 per cent
of all the world's fresh water.

The Sims 2 **is the bestselling PC game of all
time, having sold over 20 million copies.**

Starbucks is named after Starbuck, Captain
Ahab's first mate in the novel *Moby Dick*.

**Ten per cent of Britain's perfume sales take
place at Heathrow Airport.**

Toy poodles were once used as hand
warmers by the aristocracy.

**Hans Christian Andersen was so terrified
of being killed in a fire that he always
carried a piece of rope with which to
escape from burning buildings.**

In Ethiopia, hang-gliders are banned in

national parks, because antelopes mistake them for giant vultures and stampede in panic.

The famous Impressionist painter Claude Monet won enough money in a state lottery to make him financially independent, and so able to paint in the style he liked.

On average, 51 cars a year accidentally drive into the canals of Amsterdam.

When Leonardo da Vinci was young he drew a picture of a horrible monster and placed it near a window in order to surprise his father. Upon seeing the picture, his father believed it to be real until the boy showed him the truth. Da Vinci's father then enrolled his son in an art class.

The British Isles is made up of 6,289 islands (most of them off the coast of Scotland).

Sri Lankan kites can be enormous: up to nine square metres. People have to use smaller kites just to get the bigger ones into the air and they require up to 90 metres of string to fly.

Two sugar cubes rubbed together will spark.

The terminal of Hong Kong International Airport is the world's largest indoor place.

New York City has more Irish people than Dublin, Ireland; more Italians than Rome, Italy; and more Jews that Tel Aviv, Israel.

When you open a new box of crayons, the

scent you can smell is that of stearic acid – which is beef fat.

Millions of years ago, Qatar and Bahrain were joined geographically, but the two countries have drifted apart over the centuries.

The original purpose of a coffin wasn't to protect the body from animals or even from grave robbers. It was invented to keep the dead from coming back to haunt the living.

Shaka, leader of the South African Zulu tribe from 1818 to 1828, didn't trust his witch-finders, so he set them a test: he smeared his own blood on his house and told them to find the witch who did it. When they found 300 'guilty' people Shaka had the witch-finders put to death.

In the 1970 Democratic Republic of the Congo presidential election, one of the candidates received more votes than the number of registered voters.

Until fairly recently, cashiers at a chain of Chilean supermarkets wore nappies because they had to work nine-hour shifts without any breaks.

The chances of being injured by a toilet seat at some point in your life are reckoned to be one in 6,500.

In New Delhi, microchips have been inserted into the stomachs of cows so that, if lost, they can be traced and returned to their owners.

There's a free-diver named Herbert Nitsch who can hold his breath for over nine minutes.

The Palacio de Sal in Bolivia is a hotel built from salt blocks. Guests are told not to lick the walls for fear of degrading them (the walls, not the guests).

The Roman Emperor Tiberius loved cucumbers so much his gardeners invented mobile vegetable beds which could be wheeled around to capture the best of the sun (and then be wheeled indoors to keep the cucumbers warm at night).

In an experiment in which a computer program was used to diagnose sick people, it was found to be correct in 98 per cent of cases. By contrast, real-life doctors were correct in just 78 per cent of cases.

In the 1979 video game *Video Chess*, the computer could take up to ten hours to decide on a move.

People who suffer from auditory agnosia are unable to associate a sound (e.g. the noise of a washing machine) with its meaning or purpose.

Until 2010, passports issued in Vanuatu were still handwritten.

The German explorer and naturalist Alexander von Humboldt (1769 – 1859) is often described as the 'last man who knew everything'. He came across a parrot that was the sole speaker of an extinct Venezuelan language, so he recorded the last 40 words of the Artures people direct from the parrot's mouth.

***King Kong* was inspired by a 1926 trip that W. Douglas Burden, a trustee of the American Museum of Natural History, made to Indonesia to discover the truth about komodo dragons.**

Numbers

The number 1,274,953,680 uses all the digits from 1 to 9 and you can divide it exactly by any number from 1 to 16.

If you multiply 1,089 by 9 you get 9,801. It's reversed itself! This also works with 10,989 or 1,099,989 and so on.

Basically there are three types of people. Those who are good at maths... and those who are not.

The number 2,520 can be divided precisely by 1, 2, 3, 4, 5, 6, 7, 8, 9 and 10.

There is a way of writing the number 1 by using the numbers from 0 to 9 once each: 148/296 + 35/70 = 1.

Acetwothreefourfivesixseveneightnineten-jackqueenking . . . **If you add up the letters in all the names of the cards in the deck (from ace to king, excluding the joker), the total number is 52, the same as the number of cards in the deck.**

Some great trick questions to try out on your friends!

Q: If a plane crashed on the border of England and Scotland, where would they bury the survivors?
A: You don't bury survivors.

Q: If there's a frog dead in the centre of a lily pad, which is right in the middle of a

pond, which side would it jump to?
A: Neither, the frog is dead!

Q: You're a bus driver. At the first stop four people get on. At the second stop eight people get on, at the third stop two people get off, and, at the fourth stop everyone gets off. The question is, what colour are the bus driver's eyes?
A: The same as yours, you're the bus driver.

Q: A man went outside in the pouring rain with no protection, but not a hair on his head got wet . . . How come?
A: He was bald.

Q: David's father has three sons: Snap, Crackle and _____?
A: David.

Q: What has a mouth but doesn't eat, a bank with no money, a bed but doesn't sleep, and waves but has no hands?
A: A river.

Q: A cowboy rode to an inn on Friday. He stayed two nights and left on Friday. How could that be?
A: His horse was called Friday.

Q: If the red house is on the right side and if the blue house is on the left side, where's the white house?
A: Washington, DC.

Crazy helpline conversations

Customer: *I've been ringing your call centre on 0700 2300 for two days and can't get through to enquiries, can you help?*

Operator: Where did you get that number from, sir?

Customer: *It was on the door to the travel centre.*

Operator: Sir, those are our opening hours.

* * *

Tech: Ridge Hall computer assistance; may I help you?

Customer: *Yes, well, I'm having trouble with WordPerfect.*

Tech: What sort of trouble?

Customer: *Well, I was just typing along, and all of a sudden the words went away.*

Tech: Went away?

Customer: *They disappeared.*

Tech: Hmm. So what does your screen look like now?

Customer: *Nothing.*

Tech: Nothing?

Customer: *It's blank; it won't accept anything when I type.*

Tech: Are you still in WordPerfect, or did you get out?

Customer: *How do I tell?*

Tech: Can you see the 'C' prompt on the screen?

Customer: *What's a sea-prompt?*

Tech: Never mind. Can you move the cursor around on the screen?

Customer: *There isn't any cursor: I told you, it won't accept anything I type.*

Tech: Does your monitor have a power indicator?

Customer: *What's a monitor?*

Tech: It's the thing with the screen on it that looks like a TV. Does it have a little light that tells you when it's on?

Customer: *I don't know.*

Tech: Well, then look on the back of the monitor and find where the power cord goes into it. Can you see that?

Customer: . . . *Yes, I think so.*

Tech: Great! Follow the cord to the plug, and tell me if it's plugged into the wall.

Customer: . . . *Yes, it is.*

Tech: When you were behind the monitor, did you notice that there were two cables plugged into the back of it, not just one?

Customer: *No.*

Tech: Well, there are. I need you to look back there again and find the other cable.

Customer: . . . *OK, here it is.*

Tech: Follow it for me, and tell me if it's plugged securely into the back of your computer.

Customer: *I can't reach.*

Tech: Uh-huh. Well, can you see if it is?

Customer: *No.*

Tech: Even if you maybe put your knee on something and lean way over?

Customer: *Oh, it's not because I don't have the right angle – it's because it's dark.*

Tech: 'Dark'?

Customer: *Yes – the office light is off, and the only light I have is coming in from the window.*

Tech: Well, turn on the office light then.

Customer: *I can't.*

Tech: No? Why not?

Customer: *Because there's a power outage.*

Tech: A power . . . a power outage? Aha! OK, we've got it licked now. Do you still have the boxes and manuals and packing stuff your computer came in?

Customer: *Well, yes, I keep them in the closet.*

Tech: Good! Go get them, and unplug your system and pack it up just like it was when you got it. Then take it back to the store you bought it from.

Customer: *Really? Is it that bad?*

Tech: Yes, I'm afraid it is.

Customer: *Well, all right then, I suppose. What do I tell them?*

Tech: Tell them you're too stupid to own a computer.

*   *   *

Tech Support: Customer Support, this is David, may I help you?

Customer: *Hello, yes, it's me.*

Tech Support: Oh, it's me too. *[Chuckle]*

Customer: *No, Esmie. E, s, m, i, e.*

Tech Support: Oh, sorry.

*   *   *

Caller: *Does your European Breakdown Policy cover me when I am travelling in Australia?*

Operator: Doesn't the product give you a clue?

* * *

Customer: *How much does it cost to Bath on the train?*

Operator: If you can get your feet in the sink, then it's free.

* * *

Caller: *I'd like the number of the Argoed Fish Bar in Cardiff, please.*

Operator: I'm sorry, there's no listing. Is the spelling correct?

Caller: *Well, it used to be called the Bargoed Fish Bar but the 'B' fell off.*

English (well, almost) as it is written around the world (1)

In an East African newspaper:
A NEW SWIMMING POOL IS RAPIDLY TAKING SHAPE SINCE THE CONTRACTORS HAVE THROWN IN THE BULK OF THEIR WORKERS

Notice outside an American factory:
CLOSING DOWN, THANKS TO ALL OUR CUSTOMERS

Sign in a bargain basement store:
DON'T GO INTO ANOTHER SHOP TO BE CHEATED — COME IN HERE

Sign in an American chemist's:
WE DISPENSE WITH ACCURACY

Found on the instruction sheet of an American hairdryer:
WARNING: DO NOT USE IN SHOWER. NEVER USE WHILE SLEEPING

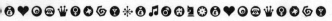

On the label of a Taiwanese shampoo:
USE REPEATEDLY FOR SEVERE DAMAGE

Found on the handle of an American
hammer:
**CAUTION: DO NOT USE THIS HAMMER TO
STRIKE ANY SOLID OBJECT**

In a Tokyo hotel:
IS FORBIDDEN TO STEAL HOTEL TOWELS PLEASE. IF YOU ARE NOT A PERSON TO DO SUCH THING IS PLEASE NOT TO READ NOTIS

On the box of a clockwork toy made in Hong Kong:
GUARANTEED TO WORK THROUGHOUT ITS USEFUL LIFE

Found on a Batman costume box in the US:
PARENT: PLEASE EXERCISE CAUTION, MASK AND CHEST PLATE ARE NOT PROTECTIVE; CAPE DOES NOT ENABLE WEARER TO FLY

From a Singapore menu:
SIR LOIN STEAK WITH POTATO CHEEPS

From Macao:
UTMOST OF CHICKEN FRIED IN BOTHER

Sign in a Paris restaurant:
WE SERVE FIVE O'CLOCK TEA AT ALL HOURS

In the lobby of a Moscow hotel across from a Russian Orthodox monastery:

YOU ARE WELCOME TO VISIT THE CEMETERY WHERE FAMOUS RUSSIAN AND SOVIET COMPOSERS, ARTISTS, AND WRITERS ARE BURIED DAILY EXCEPT THURSDAY

Notice on a soup terrine in a German cash-and-carry store:

ERBSENSUPPE / PIE SOUP

(I think it should have been 'pea soup'.

In a Paris hotel elevator:

PLEASE LEAVE YOUR VALUES AT THE FRONT DESK

On the menu of a French restaurant:

EGG — AN EXTRACT OF FOWL, PEACHED OR SUNSIDE UP

Two signs from a Majorcan shop entrance:

ENGLISH WELL TALKING
HERE SPEECHING AMERICAN

Sign in a British school:
IF YOU THINK YOU'VE GOT A PROBLEM, YOU SHOULD SEE THE HEAD

Sign outside a British nightclub:
CLOSED TONIGHT FOR SPECIAL OPENING

Advert in a British shop window:
HOME WANTED FOR FRIENDLY LABRADOR. WILL EAT ANYTHING — LOVES CHILDREN

Sign in a hotel in Madrid:
**IF YOU WISH DISINFECTION ENACTED
IN YOUR PRESENCE, CRY OUT FOR THE
CHAMBERMAID**

In a Budapest zoo:
**PLEASE DO NOT FEED THE ANIMALS. IF YOU
HAVE ANY SUITABLE FOOD, GIVE IT TO THE
GUARD ON DUTY**

In the office of a Roman doctor:
SPECIALIST IN WOMEN AND OTHER DISEASES

In a Swiss mountain inn:
SPECIAL TODAY – NO ICE CREAM

In an Austrian hotel catering to skiers:
**NOT TO PERAMBULATE THE CORRIDORS IN
THE HOURS OF REPOSE IN THE BOOTS OF
ASCENSION**

On the menu of a Polish hotel:
**SALAD A FIRM'S OWN MAKE; LIMPID RED
BEET SOUP WITH CHEESY DUMPLINGS IN**

THE FORM OF A FINGER; ROASTED DUCK LET LOOSE; BEEF RASHERS BEATEN UP IN THE COUNTRY PEOPLE'S FASHION

In a Leipzig lift:
DO NOT ENTER THE LIFT BACKWARDS, AND ONLY WHEN LIT UP

In a hotel in Athens:
VISITORS ARE EXPECTED TO COMPLAIN AT THE OFFICE BETWEEN THE HOURS OF 9 AND 11 A.M. DAILY

In a Vienna hotel:
IN CASE OF FIRE, DO YOUR UTMOST TO ALARM THE HOTEL PORTER

From the *Soviet Weekly*:
THERE WILL BE A MOSCOW EXHIBITION OF ARTS BY 150,000 SOVIET REPUBLIC PAINTERS AND SCULPTORS. THESE WERE EXECUTED OVER THE PAST TWO YEARS

From a Yugoslavian elevator:
LET US KNOW ABOUT AN UNFICIENCY AS WELL AS LEAKING ON THE SERVICE. OUR UTMOST WILL IMPROVE IT

From a tailor's shop in Rhodes:
ORDER YOUR SUMMERS SUIT. BECAUSE IS BIG RUSH WE WILL EXECUTE CUSTOMERS IN STRICT ROTATION

Portuguese patent agent:
IT WILL NOT BE NECESSARY TO STATE THE NAME AND ADDRESS OF THE INVENTOR IF THE APPLICANT IS NOT HIMSELF

On a Soviet ship in the Black Sea:
HELPSAVERING APPARATA IN EMERGINGS BEHOLD MANY WHISTLES! ASSOCIATE THE STRINGING APPARATA ABOUT THE BOSOMS AND MEET BEHIND. FLEE THEN TO THE INDIFFERENT LIFESAVERING SHIPPEN OBEDIENCING THE INSTRUCTS OF THE VESSEL CHEF

Sign in a furniture shop:
WE STAND BEHIND EVERY BED WE SELL

Sign in a hotel lift:
PLEASE DO NOT USE THIS LIFT WHEN IT IS NOT WORKING

Sign in a dry-cleaner's:
IF YOU FEEL WE HAVE FAILED YOU IN ANY WAY WE SHALL BE ONLY TOO PLEASED TO DO IT AGAIN AT NO EXTRA CHARGE

Sign in a jewellery shop:
OUR GIFTS WILL NOT LAST LONG AT THESE PRICES

Sign in a beauty parlour:
EARS PIERCED WHILE YOU WAIT. PAY FOR TWO AND GET ANOTHER ONE PIERCED FREE

Music

Mozart wrote a piano piece that required the player to use both hands and his nose.

The earliest example of musical notation comes from 200 BC Sumeria.

Three Gershwin songs, *I Got Rhythm*, *Nice Work if You Can Get It* and *I'm About to Become a Mother*, all contain the phrase 'Who could ask for anything more?'

The Oscar-winning actress Kate Winslet had a Top Ten hit with *What If* in 2001.

The well-known song *She'll Be Comin' Round the Mountain (When She Comes)*

was based on the hymn *When the Chariot Comes.*

Michael Bublé's grandfather was a plumber, and would fix problems at nightclubs for free if the owners allowed Bublé to sing there.

Waterfalls

At 979 metres tall, with a clear drop of 807 metres, the world's highest waterfall is the Angel Falls in Venezuela. It's 20 times taller than Niagara Falls, and its height is so great that the water is turned into mist by the wind before it reaches the ground.

The Angel Falls are named after the American pilot Jimmy Angel, whose plane got stuck at the top of the waterfall in 1937. It took him and his companions 11 days to climb down the side of the waterfall.

The second highest waterfall is Tugela in South Africa (947 metres). Norway boasts the world's third and fourth highest waterfalls (Utigord at 800 metres and Monge at 774 metres).

Christmas

Christmas pies – aka mince pies – were banned by Oliver Cromwell and the Puritans in 1657 on the basis that Christmas should be a serious time with absolutely no fun or indulgence.

The phenomenon of retailers promoting Christmas shopping earlier and earlier every year is known as 'Christmas Creep'.

The average British mother spends 13 days preparing for Christmas.

Two thirds of office workers receive corporate Christmas cards from people they don't know.

In the 19th century, Christmas cards were delivered on Christmas Day itself.

Every Christmas we in the UK use around 83 square kilometres of wrapping paper.

Unusual collective names

In some cases there are alternative names to these – but I've picked the more exotic!

A sounder of boars

An obstinacy of buffaloes

A caravan of camels

A quiver of cobras

An intrusion of cockroaches

A float of crocodiles

A murder of crows

A dule of doves

A paddling of ducks

A parade of elephants

A gang of elks

A cast of falcons

A business of ferrets

A charm of finches

A skulk of flamingos

A tower of giraffes

An implausibilty of gnus

A troubling of goldfish

A leash of greyhounds

A husk of hares

A kettle of hawks

An array of hedgehogs

A bloat of hippopotamuses

A parcel of hogs

A smack of jellyfish

A mob of kangaroos

An exultation of larks

A leap of leopards

A gulp of magpies

A mischief of mice

A labour of moles

A troop of monkeys

A romp of otters

A parliament of owls

A company of parrots

A parcel of penguins

A bouquet of pheasants

A crash of rhinos

A clamour of rooks

A host of sparrows

A murmuration of starlings

A mustering of storks

A lamentation of swans

An ambush of tigers

A knot of toads

A gang of turkeys

A carpet of vultures

A huddle of walruses

A descent of woodpeckers

A zeal of zebras

Books

In 1097 Trotula, a midwife in the Italian town of Salerno wrote a book called *The Diseases of Women*, which was used in medical schools for 600 years.

The Bible has been translated into 2,200 languages and dialects.

Before settling on the name of Tiny Tim for the name of his character in *A Christmas Carol*, Charles Dickens considered – and rejected – Little Larry, Puny Pete and Small Sam.

It is estimated that of the millions of cookery books owned in Britain, more than a third have never been opened.

The people of Iceland read more books than any other nationality in the world. It must be all those long, cold evenings!

Banned books

The Catcher in the Rye by J. D. Salinger (1951): banned in Boron, California, in 1989 because of the word 'goddamn'. It was also banned in another US state because of the words 'hell' and 'for Chrissake'. This is probably the most famous work of fiction never to have been turned into a feature film.

The Adventures of Tom Sawyer by Mark Twain (1876): banned by several London libraries (in politically correct Labour-controlled boroughs) in the mid-1980s on account of the book's alleged racism and sexism.

Black Beauty by Anna Sewell(1877): banned by the African country Namibia in the 1970s because the government took offence at its supposedly racist title.

The *Noddy* series by Enid Blyton (1949 – 63): banned by several British libraries in the 1960s – along with other Enid Blyton

books – because some thought the books were not good for children.

The Grapes of Wrath by John Steinbeck (1939): banned from schools in Iowa, USA, in 1980 after a parent complained that the classic novel – by the Nobel Prize winner – was 'vulgar and obscene'. Steinbeck's other famous novel, *Of Mice and Men*, has been banned in other US states for similar reasons.

The *Billy Bunter* series by Frank Richards (1947 – 67): banned from British libraries in the 1970s in case it led children to tease overweight schoolmates.

On the Origin of Species by Charles Darwin (1859): banned in several US states (especially in the Christian Fundamentalist South) through the years – but particularly before the Second World War – as it contradicts the Bible's account of Creation. Desmond Morris's book *The Naked Ape* (1967), which compares human behaviour to that of other species, has been banned from one or two US libraries on the same basis. Darwin's book was also banned by the USSR because it was 'immoral'.

More unintentionally funny (but genuine!) newspaper headlines

BANK DRIVE-IN WINDOW BLOCKED BY BOARD

HERE'S HOW YOU CAN LICK DOBERMAN'S LEG SORES

COUPLE SLAIN: POLICE SUSPECT HOMICIDE

DOG THAT BIT 2 PEOPLE ORDERED TO LEAVE TOWN

ENRAGED BULL INJURES FARMER WITH AXE

FILMING IN CEMETERY ANGERS RESIDENTS

GAS RIG MEN GRILLED BY VILLAGERS

IF STRIKE ISN'T SETTLED QUICKLY, IT MAY LAST A WHILE

KILLER SENTENCED TO DIE FOR SECOND TIME IN 10 YEARS

LARGER KANGAROOS LEAP FARTHER, RESEARCHERS FIND

LAWMEN FROM MEXICO BARBECUE GUESTS

MAGISTRATES ACT TO KEEP THEATRES OPEN

FACTORY ORDERS DIP

MAN FOUND DEAD IN CEMETERY

MAN RUN OVER BY FREIGHT TRAIN DIES

NO WATER SO FIREMEN IMPROVISED

OFFICIAL: ONLY RAIN WILL CURE DROUGHT

PLOT TO KILL OFFICER HAD VICIOUS SIDE

GIRL KICKED BY HORSE UPGRADED TO STABLE

POLICE MOVE IN BOOK CASE

POLICE RECOVER STOLEN HAMSTER, ARREST 3

POSTMEN AWARDED A £2 MILLION PAY RISE

PROPERLY DRAFTED WILL REDUCES ANXIETY AFTER DEATH

CORONER REPORTS ON WOMAN'S DEATH WHILE RIDING HORSE

QUARTER OF A MILLION CHINESE LIVE ON WATER

SCHOOL CHILDREN MARCH OVER NEW TEACHERS

STAR'S BROKEN LEG HITS BOX OFFICE

POLICE NAB STUDENT WITH PAIR OF PLIERS

SUPERTRAIN TALKS

THREATENING LETTERS — MAN ASKS FOR LONG SENTENCE

THREE AMBULANCES TAKE BLAST VICTIM TO HOSPITAL

VOLUNTARY WORKERS STRIKE FOR HIGHER PAY

BODIES NEEDED TO LOOK AFTER GRAVEYARD

CRIME: SHERIFF ASKS FOR 13.7% INCREASE

DEAF COLLEGE OPENS DOORS TO HEARING

DEBATE ABOUT HANGING SUSPENDED

FOUR BATTERED IN FISH AND CHIP SHOP

GOLDFISH IS SAVED FROM DROWNING

IRAQI HEAD SEEKS ARMS

JURY SUSPECTS FOUL PLAY IN DEATH OF MAN SHOT, BURNED & BURIED IN SHALLOW GRAVE

MAN DENIES HE COMMITTED SUICIDE

MAN MINUS EAR WAIVES HEARING

NUNS FORGIVE BREAK-IN, ASSAULT SUSPECT

PASSENGERS HIT BY CANCELLED TRAINS

PATIENT AT DEATH'S DOOR — DOCTORS PULL HIM THROUGH

PLANE TOO CLOSE TO GROUND, CRASH PROBE TOLD

PRISONERS ESCAPE AFTER EXECUTION

RED TAPE HOLDS UP NEW BRIDGES

STUDY REVEALS THOSE WITHOUT INSURANCE DIE MORE OFTEN

TEACHER DIES; BOARD ACCEPTS HIS RESIGNATION

THIEVES STEAL BURGLAR ALARM

NEW HOUSING FOR ELDERLY NOT YET DEAD

NEW AUTOS TO HIT 5 MILLION

12 ON THEIR WAY TO CRUISE AMONG DEAD IN PLANE CRASH

GENETIC ENGINEERING SPLITS SCIENTISTS

AMERICAN SHIPS HEAD TO LIBYA

DENTIST RECEIVES PLAQUE

Pure trivia

'Ape's Laugh', 'Smoked Ox', 'Chimney-Sweep, and 'Dying Monkey' were the names of 16th-century lipsticks.

About 40 per cent of the listeners of BBC Radio 4's *Woman's Hour* are men.

A couple named Richard and Carol Roble re-married each other 56 times.

In its infancy, the Pepsi-Cola Company was declared bankrupt three times.

Pablo Picasso and Louis Pasteur both had Paris Métro stations named after them.

23 per cent of all photocopier faults worldwide are caused by people copying their buttocks.

The word 'and' appears 46,277 times in the Bible.

Beethoven took hay baths to remedy the swelling he used to get in his legs.

The US Government spent $277,000 on pickle research in 1993.

In 1907 an ad campaign for Kellogg's Corn Flakes offered a free box of cereal to any woman who winked at her grocer.

In Britain, about ten people a week go to hospital because of injuries suffered while playing Wii games.

The Greek word for love is *philadelphia* – which is also the name of a major American city.

American tobacco auctioneers can speak at up to 400 words per minute.

The longest rendering of a national anthem was *God Save the King*, performed by a German military band on the platform at Rathenau station in Brandenburg, on 9 February 1909. King Edward VII was struggling inside the train to get into his German Field-Marshal uniform, so the band had to play the anthem 17 consecutive times.

St Brigid of Ireland, a sixth-century abbess of Kildare, was said to be able to transform her used bathwater into beer.

The Japanese electronic games company Nintendo, which first started trading in 1889, translates into English as 'leave luck to heaven'.

David Warren, the man who invented the

flight data recorder (or 'black box'), was buried in a casket bearing a label that read *Flight Recorder Inventor; Do Not Open*

In Australia, Burger King is called Hungry Jack's.

Snail races usually start with the words 'Ready, steady, slow!'

There's a Malaysian cult that worships a giant teapot, which they believe symbolizes 'the healing purity of water'.

In a cemetery in Brighton, a Mr Bacon is buried next to a Mrs Egg.

Two days after winning his first ever Wimbledon title, Roger Federer was presented with a milking cow as a gift from tournament organizers in Gstaad, Switzerland. He named her Juliette.

Strange – but genuine – jobs

Can catcher – person who has to make

sure that cans at the end of a conveyor belt don't crash into each other and get dented.

Foot straightener – person who screws the feet on clock dials into place.

Weed farmer – person who deliberately grows weeds for use in research.

Toe puncher – person who looks after the toe-punching machine which flattens the toe seams of socks.

Sniffer – person who sniffs people's underarms to test the effectiveness of deodorants.

Same words – different pronunciation!

Read these aloud to see just how odd the English language is!

The bandage was wound around the wound.

The farm was used to produce produce.

The dump was so full that it had to refuse more refuse.

We must polish the Polish Furniture.

He could lead if he would get the lead out.

The soldier decided to desert his dessert in the desert.

Since there is no time like the present, he thought it was time to present the present.

A bass was painted on the head of the bass drum.

When shot at, the dove dove into the bushes.

I did not object to the object.

The insurance was invalid for the invalid.

There was a row among the oarsmen about how to row.

They were too close to the door to close it.

The buck does funny things when the does are present.

A seamstress and a sewer fell down into a sewer line.

To help with planting, the farmer taught his sow to sow.

The wind was too strong to wind the sail.

Upon seeing the tear in the painting I shed a tear.

I had to subject the subject to a series of tests.

How can I intimate this to my most intimate friend?

Movies

More popcorn is sold during scary movies than during comedies.

'Smithee' is a pseudonym that film-makers use when they don't want their names to appear in the credits.

Sharon Stone gave up part of her salary to

get Leonardo DiCaprio cast in the western *The Quick and the Dead*.

As an 18-year-old, Cate Blanchett was on holiday in Egypt and appeared as a film extra in a crowd scene, cheering for an American boxer who was losing to an Egyptian. She hated it so much she walked off the set.

For the 1959 thriller *The Tingler*, theatres were rigged with buzzers under the seats to scare viewers at key moments in the film.

The movie *Earthquake* featured Sensurround, which shook the theatre seats.

The Exuma Islands have been used as a location for two different James Bond films: *Thunderball* and *Never Say Never Again*.

The most used line in the movies is 'Let's get out of here.'

In the film *E.T.* (1982), the sound of E.T. walking was made by someone squishing her hands in jelly.

In *The Bridge on the River Kwai* (1957), Alec Guinness – who won an Oscar for his role – had his name spelled with just one 'n' in the final credits.

Kevin Spacey requests a ping-pong table in his room whenever he's on location.

The film director David Lynch always leaves one shoelace untied. No reason: it's just something he does!

Ground crew get their revenge!

Here are some maintenance complaints/problems made by pilots from the Australian airline QANTAS . . . and the amusing responses of the engineers and ground crew!

(P – The problem, as logged by the pilot.)
(S – The solution, as logged by the engineers.)

P – Left inside main tyre almost needs replacement.
S – Almost replaced left inside main tyre.

P – Test flight OK, except auto-land very rough.
S – Auto-land not installed on this aircraft.

P – Something loose in cockpit.
S – Something tightened in cockpit.

P – Evidence of leak on right main landing gear.
S – Evidence removed.

P – DME volume unbelievably loud.
S – Volume set to more believable level.

P – Friction locks cause throttle levers to stick.
S – That's what they are there for!

P – IFF inoperative.
S – IFF always inoperative in OFF mode.

P – Suspected crack in windscreen.
S – Suspect you're right.

P – Number three engine missing.
S – Engine found on right wing after brief search.

has no past history of suicides.

ft his white blood cells at
ital.

medical history has been
nsignificant with only a 40-
t gain in the past three days.

from her toes down.

moist and dry.

onstant, infrequent

rt and unresponsive.

she had been constipated
life, until she got a divorce.

ient today, who is still under
ysical therapy.

teenage children but no
ities.

t pale but present.

P – Aircraft handles funny.
S – Aircraft warned to 'Straighten Up, Fly Right, and Be Serious.'

P – Target radar hums.
S – Reprogrammed target radar with words.

P – Mouse in cockpit.
S – Cat installed.

Some countries and their most popular surnames

Austria: Gruber

Canada: Johnson

Costa Rica: Jiménez

Czech Republic: Novak

Finland: Virtanen

Georgia: Beridze

Germany: Müller

Italy: Rossi

Latvia: Berzins

Malta: Borg

Norway: Hansen

The Philippines: Santos

Singapore

Slovakia:

Slovenia:

Sweden:

Turkey:

Funny
made
pati

Patier
side f

On th
on th

Disc
per

The

The patient

Patient has l
another hosp

Patient's pas
remarkably i
pound weigh

She is numb

The skin was

Occasional, c
headaches.

Patient was al

She stated tha
for most of he

I saw your pat
our car for ph

Patient has two
other abnorma

Skin: Somewha

Patient was seen in consultation by Dr Blank, who felt we should sit on the abdomen, and I agree.

By the time he was admitted, his rapid heart stopped, and he was feeling better.

The patient was in his usual state of good health until his aeroplane ran out of gas and crashed.

When she fainted, her eyes rolled around the room.

Patient was released to outpatient department without dressing.

The patient expired on the floor uneventfully.

By the time he was admitted, his rapid heart had stopped, and he was feeling better.

She slipped on the ice and apparently her legs went in separate directions in early December.

The patient left the hospital feeling much better except for her original complaints.

She is numb from her toes down.

She was divorced last April. No other serious illness.

Apparently the mother resented the fact that she was born in her forties.

Countries and their symbols

Some countries have many national symbols but here's a selection:

Argentina – Puma

Austria – Edelweiss (a mountain flower)

Bangladesh – Water lily

Bolivia – Llama

Bulgaria – Lion

Canada – Maple leaf

Colombia – Condor

England – Rose, Bulldog

Eritrea – Camel (During Eritrea's war of independence from Ethiopia, the camel was the main means of transportation for moving food supplies, arms, ammunition and people across the country.)

Germany – Black eagle

Guatemala – The quetzal (A bird that signifies freedom because it dies in captivity: it's also the name of the Guatemalan currency.)

Iceland – Falcon

India – Lotus

Monaco – Carnation

Nepal – Cow

New Zealand – Kiwi bird

Pakistan – Jasmine

Singapore – Orchid

Slovakia – Gothic shield (with a silver double cross mounted on the central peak of three blue mountains, which represent the three ranges of the Carpathian mountains).

South Africa – Springbok

United Arab Emirates – Arabian horse

Human beings

Your ribs move about five million times a year (i.e. every time you breathe).

The pupil of the eye expands as much as 45 per cent when a person looks at something pleasing to them.

15 million blood cells are produced and destroyed in the human body every second.

If you squeezed out all the bacteria from your intestines, you could almost fill up a mug.

Each red blood cell lives an average of four months and travels between the lungs and other tissues 75,000 times before returning to the bone marrow to die.

Your heart rate can rise as much as 30 per cent during a yawn.

We have no sense of smell when we're asleep. And this is the fact that gave the book it's title!

Children dream more frequently than adults.

Women's hair is about half the diameter of men's.

During his or her lifetime, the average human will grow 590 miles of hair.

When you're wide awake, alert and mentally active, you're still never more than 25 per cent aware of what various parts of your body are doing.

The human kidney consists of over one

million little tubes with a total length of about 40 miles in both kidneys.

Your hearing is less sharp if you eat too much.

Girls learn to talk earlier, use sentences earlier, and learn to read more quickly than boys.

People with blue eyes are better able to see in the dark.

Redheads require more anaesthesia to 'go under' than people withother hair colours do.

Men have more car accidents than women, but drive more miles. Women have more accidents per mile driven.

Athlete's Foot is the most common skin infection. It's caused by a fungus that causes the skin between the toes to peel off.

Girls are one-and-a-half times more likely than boys to be double-jointed.

Only one per cent of bacteria cause disease in humans.

Women blink nearly twice as often as men.

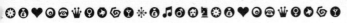

The lens of the eye continues to grow throughout a person's life.

One out of 20 people has an extra rib.

The average adult has between 40 and 50 billion fat cells.

Every square centimetre of the human body has an average of 13 million bacteria on it.

Your brain will stop growing in size when you are about 15 years old.

The human brain is capable of recording more than 86 million bits of information per day.

Human blood travels 60,000 miles (96,540 kilometres) per day on its journey through the body.

The mineral content, porosity and general make-up of human bone is nearly identical to some species of South Pacific coral. The two are so alike that plastic surgeons are

using the coral in facial reconstructions, to replace lost human bone.

The total amount that the average person will eat in a lifetime is equivalent of the weight of 60 elephants.

Your body gives off enough heat in half an hour to bring a litre of water to the boil.

About ten billion tiny scales of skin come off your body every day. These scales don't weigh very much but, over a lifetime, each of us sheds around 20 kilograms of dead skin.

Human sweat contains a chemical that is the same as a wasp's poison. That's the poison from a wasp and not the poison used to kill it.

According to Sigmund Freud, civilization only became possible when men resisted the urge to put out their camp fires by peeing on them.

Around the world (1)

Kulang, China, has seven centres for recycled toothpicks. People bring used toothpicks to the recycling centres and

are paid the equivalent of 25 pence per pound weight.

Floor-cleaning products in Venezuela have ten times the pine fragrance of British floor cleaners, as Venezuelans prefer the stronger smell.

Of all the land on earth, 7.6 per cent is currently being farmed – half the amount that could be farmed.

More than three billion people in the world are malnourished – that's to say they don't have enough food. This is the highest number of hungry people in recorded history.

70 per cent of computer virus writers work under contract for organized crime syndicates.

67 per cent of the world's illiterate adults are female.

At Tokyo's Keio University Hospital, 30 per cent of the outpatients diagnosed with

throat polyps attributed the cause of the affliction to singing karaoke.

When Inuit babies have colds, their mothers suck the snot out of their noses.

The University of al-Karaouine, Morocco, is the world's oldest operating university. It was founded in the year 859 and is still running.

Some Hondurans believe that foods and herbs are either 'hot' or 'cold'. Some of the hot foods are coffee, oranges and beef. Cold foods include coconuts, bananas, salt and seafood. When someone is ill, hot or cold foods or herbs may be prescribed, depending on the illness.

In Qatar, the separation of men and women extends to places of prayer, government offices, shops and even lifts.

In Japan, they have a problem with karoshi – which literally means 'death from overwork'. The high pressure of the Japanese workplace has led to a number of deaths from stress-related disorders. This could have something to do with the fact that the average Japanese worker reportedly takes only half his or her holiday time each year.

Women in Senegal spend an average of 17.5 hours a week just collecting water from wells.

In Vietnam, the surname is written first, the middle name second and the 'first' name last.

In the United Arab Emirates, people from other countries have to return to their country of origin once they get to retirement age.

There are no tall apartment blocks on Grenada because there's a law that development may not rise above the height of a coconut palm.

In Mongolia, all houses are privately owned: there's no state or social housing.

On average, the people of India spend more time reading than any other people in the world.

Kazakhstan is the largest landlocked country in the world. It's also the ninth largest country of all but, thanks to its terrain (the desert-like steppes), there are only six people per square kilometre.

Uzbekistan is the largest doubly landlocked country in the world. This means that it's surrounded on all sides by other landlocked countries.

Animals

Unlike most cats, tigers love the water and can easily swim three or four miles.

Wolf packs used to be found in all the forests of Europe, and in 1420 and 1438, wolves roamed the streets of Paris.

The highest paid animal actors are bears, which can earn $20,000 a day.

While drug-sniffing dogs are trained to bark like crazy, and act aggressively at the first whiff of drugs, bomb-sniffing dogs are trained to act passively in case they set off a motion sensor or a noise sensor, or any number of other things that might go 'kablooie'.

Rats prefer boiled sweets to cheese.

There are wolves in Sweden – but only about 100 in the whole country.

Cats spend 85 per cent of their day doing nothing.

The average cat costs its owner £7,000 over its lifetime (compared with £20,000 for a dog).

Dachshunds were bred to fight badgers in their dens.

Howler monkeys are well named as they're the noisiest land animals. Their calls can be heard over two miles away.

The name 'poodle' derives from the

German *pudeln*, meaning 'to splash in water'.

Puerto Rico has few native mammals but does boast a horse called the Paso Fino. Known as the horse of the Spanish conquistadores, it has a smooth natural gait that makes riding it 'as smooth as glass'.

The world's smallest mammal (where skull size is the defining factor) is the bumblebee bat of Thailand.

Tasmanian Devils can eat 40 per cent of their own body weight in 30 minutes.

Tortoises drink water through their noses.

A squirrel can use its tail as a parachute should it fall from a tree. The tail can also be used to cushion a hard landing and to communicate with other squirrels.

The word 'squirrel' comes from the Greek word meaning 'shadow-tailed', because

the squirrel uses its tail to keep warm or shade itself from the sun.

The heart of a mouse beats 650 times per minute!

Elephants are 70 per cent water.

The oldest pig in the world lived to the age of 68.

Before going into its winter hibernation, a dormouse breathes at the rate of 260 breaths a second.

Rats can tell the difference between two human languages.

Polar bears can eat more than 50 kilos of meat in one sitting.

Billy goats urinate on their own heads to smell more attractive to females.

Rats have been trained to sniff out landmines. They have a nose for them, and are too light to trigger off an explosion. In

the First World War, doves and rats were often sent into tunnels behind enemy lines to check for poisonous gas. It's believed that around 16 million animals assisted the armed forces.

During the Second World War elephants were used in Burma (now Myanmar) to build roads and transport humans.

Cats were used on board ship in both wars, and in the trenches of the First World War to help get rid of rats.

Rattlesnakes use their skin to feel the body heat of other animals.

Not only can a leopard kill an animal three times its weight, it can then carry its prey up a tree and out of the reach of other animals – especially scavengers like hyenas and jackals.

You can tell the gender of a horse by its teeth. Males have 40 while females have 36.

There is no single cat called the panther. The name can be applied to the leopard, the puma, the cougar and the jaguar.

Sand can form up to half of the stomach contents of a Screaming Hairy Armadillo.

The Dickin Medal, which was created in 1943 by Maria Dickin, is awarded to animals for acts of bravery. So far only 60 animals have received the Dickin Medal: 32 pigeons, 24 dogs, three horses and one cat.

Sea life

Lobsters are scared of octopuses. The sight of one makes a lobster freeze.

The national fish of Hawaii is the Humuhumunukunukuapua'a (or the 'reef triggerfish', as it is also known).

Alligator eggs that are incubated at temperatures of 32 – 34°C (90 – 93°F) will be male. Temperatures of 28 – 30°C (82 – 86°F) result in females. Intermediate temps yield a mix of males and females.

Bull sharks have been known to kill hippos in rivers.

Every day, a baby grey whale drinks enough milk to fill more than 2,000 baby bottles. Luckily for the oceans, they don't actually use baby bottles . . .

When common eels lay their eggs, they die.

The lungfish is able to survive buried in dried-up mud throughout the dry season because it can breathe in air through its lungs.

An octopus's arm typically has about 200 suckers. When threatened, it can detach an arm to confuse an enemy. The arm will regrow in a few months.

Many reptiles can replace limbs or tails if they're lost or damaged, but only the aquatic newt has the ability to regenerate the lens of its eye.

The grey whale has a series of up to 180 fringed overlapping plates hanging from each side of its upper jaw. This is where its teeth would be located if it had any.

The basking shark's liver, which accounts for up to a quarter of its body weight, runs the entire length of the abdominal cavity and is reckoned to play a role in keeping it buoyant.

The pineapplefish is also known as the

'port-and-starboard light fish' because
the two luminescent organs on its head
resemble a ship's navigation lights.

**Sharks have very strong jaws. They can
bite other animals in half – even those
with tough shells, such as turtles.**

The New Zealand sea lion is a surprisingly
good climber.

**The zebra shark is striped in its youth but
spotted when mature.**

Birds

Emus lay emerald-coloured eggs.

Over 10,000 birds a year die from
smashing into windows.

**There are about 40 different muscles in a
bird's wing.**

If a seagull consumed Alka-Seltzer, its
stomach would explode.

The nest of the bald eagle can weigh well over a ton.

Emus have double-plumed feathers.

A woodchuck breathes just ten times during hibernation.

Magpies don't just eat roadkill. They've also been known to carry off live chickens. Sounds awful, but it's not really that different to the way we go off to the supermarket to pick up a chicken for Sunday lunch.

Some bird species, usually flightless ones, have only a lower eyelid, whereas pigeons use upper and lower lids to blink.

The Puerto Rican parrot, which makes its home in hollowed-out tree trunks in the mountains, is one of the most endangered birds in the world.

Grebes plunge as deep as 30 metres and can stay underwater for as long as three minutes. While down there they snare fish,

which they swallow alive – head first.

Penguins have many natural predators, including birds, whales, mammals and, occasionally, fish.

The African owl isn't an owl; it's a pigeon.

The dove is mentioned in the Bible over 50 times – more than any other bird.

The nests of white-winged widowbirds are always built by the males.

Creepy-crawlies

The honeybee can differentiate between various people.

Grasshoppers have white blood.

Insects don't make noises with voices, but by rapidly moving their wings.

Slugs can fertilize their own eggs.

If two flies were left to reproduce without

predators or other limitations for one year, the resulting mass of flies would be the size of the earth.

I told you not to invite all the family around for lunch!

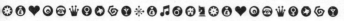

A large swarm of locusts can eat up to 85,000 tons of corn a day.

The biggest spider in the world weighed 122 grams and was captured in Suriname in 1985.

There are up to eight million worms in the soil of each hectare of forest.

Some crickets burrow megaphone-like tunnels that help transport the sound of their chirps as far as 600 metres.

Flatworms reproduce by splitting into two new worms after mating.

Termite nests are sometimes used in the construction industry because the dirt is dust-free.

The most poisonous spider is not the black widow, but the wingless daddy longlegs – although its fangs can't pierce human skin so it poses no threat.

Most snails are hermaphrodites,

meaning they have both female and male reproductive organs.

Australian termites have been known to build mounds six metres high and at least 30 metres wide.

When it's startled by a possible predator, an ant raises its abdomen. This sends a signal to other ants in the colony, and all the other ants raise their abdomens too.

Woodlice are vulnerable to a host of predators, so they secrete unpleasant fluids that make them less tasty. Alas, it's not that effective and many of them get eaten anyway.

In the 19th century, a man in Nebraska in the US spotted a swarm of Rocky Mountain locusts (now extinct). He reported that the swarm averaged a half-mile in height (some locusts were more than a mile above the ground) and was 100 miles wide and 300 miles long. The swarm moved at about five miles per hour

in the air and continued to pass for six hours. Having worked out the number of locusts per square metre, he was able to calculate that the swarm had consisted of some 124,000,000,000 locusts, each capable of devouring its own body weight in crops and vegetation.

The woodworm beetle gets its name from the practice of the female, which deposits some 50 eggs onto wood. The eggs hatch after three or four weeks, and the larvae then tunnel into the nearest piece of wood (in a house, this is usually between the joints of wooden furniture). The larvae remain in the wood, chomping away, until they are fully grown – which takes between two and five years. Then they eat away to create a small chamber in which they can pupate. After a few weeks the adult beetles eat their way to the surface and fly out, leaving behind large exit holes. These tiny creatures do a huge amount of damage compared to their size.

The first flight on earth was undoubtedly made by an insect.

Long ago, before the months were named after Roman emperors, the month we now call July was called 'worm month' in certain parts of northern Europe. The worms concerned were blowfly larvae or maggots, and it reminds us of what a problem it must have been to keep meat fit for human consumption during the summer months.

In Australia, the warm winds blow swarms of flies from the north down to the south – sometimes over hundreds of miles in a day. This explains why hordes of flies can appear as if from nowhere.

Unlike most insects, the female earwig watches over her eggs until they hatch and then protects her young.

Burying beetles are even more unusual among insects in that both the males and females take care of their offspring.

You know how people put mothballs on their clothes – especially when they're not going to be wearing them for a while? In fact, it is the larvae of moths that damage cloths, not the moths themselves.

Adult earwigs can float in water for up to 24 hours.

Female tarantulas have been known to live for up to 30 years. Males rarely live longer than a few months.

The caterpillar of the Polyphemus moth can eat 86,000 times its birth weight in less than two months.

We humans have managed to get the honeybee to work for us, but the silkworm moth is the only truly domesticated insect as it would cease to exist without human care.

The North American black and orange monarch butterfly is the only insect known to be capable of flying over 2,500 miles. This remarkable insect flies between continents during its migration.

Only fully-grown male crickets can chirp.

The mayfly is the only insect that has two adult stages.

The firefly is the only insect that produces its own energy.

A fly's eyes don't have any eyelids, so flies rub them with their feet to keep them clean.

The ghost moth can whistle through its tongue.

Genuine job performance reviews

Since my last report, this employee has reached rock bottom – and has started to dig.

His men would follow him anywhere – but only out of morbid curiosity.

I would not allow this employee to breed.

This employee is really not so much of a 'has-been', but more of a definite 'won't be'.

Works well when under constant supervision and cornered like a rat in a trap.

When she opens her mouth, it seems that it is only to change feet.

He would be out of his depth in a parking-lot puddle.

This young lady has delusions of adequacy.

He sets low personal standards and then consistently fails to achieve them.

This employee is depriving a village somewhere of an idiot.

This employee should go far . . . and the sooner he starts, the better.

A gross ignoramus – 144 times worse than an ordinary ignoramus.

He would argue with a sign post.

He brings a lot of joy whenever he leaves the room.

When his IQ reaches 50, he should sell.

If you see two people talking and one looks bored – he's the other one.

A photographic memory but with the lens cover glued on.

Donated his brain to science before he was done using it.

Gates are down, the lights are flashing, but the train isn't coming.

Has two brains: one is lost and the other is out looking for it.

If he were any more stupid, he'd have to be watered twice a week.

If you give him a penny for his thoughts, you'd get change.

The wheel is turning, but the hamster is dead.

More great April Fool's Day pranks

1915: In the middle of the First World War, a French aviator flew over a German military camp and dropped what appeared to be a huge bomb. The German soldiers scattered in all directions, but the bomb didn't go off. Very nervously, the soldiers tiptoed towards the bomb which, in fact, wasn't a bomb but a large football with a note tied to it reading 'April Fool!'

1959: The residents of Wellingborough, Northamptonshire, woke up to find that someone had left a trail of white footprints painted all along the main street. When the footsteps stopped they found the words 'I must fly'.

1962: Back when there was only one black-and-white television channel in Sweden, the station's technical expert, Kjell Stensson, announced on the news that viewers could convert their existing TV sets to colour. All they had to do was to pull a nylon stocking over their screens . . . something he then demonstrated on screen. Thousands of people were taken in. Regular colour broadcasts in Sweden started eight years later: on 1 April – yes, honestly! – 1970.

1965: A Danish newspaper reported that their parliament had passed a new law requiring all dogs to be painted white. Why? To improve safety on the roads by enabling drivers to see any dogs that were out and about at night.

1965: BBC TV featured an interview with a professor who, it was claimed, had just invented a device called 'smellovision' which would allow viewers to experience smells from the television studio. The professor proceeded to offer a demonstration by brewing coffee and slicing up some onions. A number of viewers called in claiming that they had experienced these scents as if they were right there in the studio with him.

1975: An Australian news programme announced that the country was planning to convert to 'metric time' in which there would be 100 seconds to the minute, 100 minutes to the hour, and 20-hour days. In addition, seconds would become millidays, minutes would become centidays, and hours would become decidays. The town hall in Adelaide was shown with a new ten-hour metric clock face. The programme received many calls from viewers who believed the story.

1980: *Soldier* magazine reported that the black fur on the bearskin helmets worn by the Irish Guards at Buckingham Palace kept growing and needed to be trimmed regularly. The article quoted a Major

Ursa who said: 'Bears hibernate in the winter and the amazing thing is that in the spring the skins really start to sprout.' An accompanying photo showed guardsmen sitting in an army barbershop having their helmets trimmed. A national newspaper fell for the report and ran it as a straight story.

1981: The *Daily Mail* ran a story about an unfortunate Japanese long-distance runner, Kimo Nakajimi, who had misunderstood the rules of the London Marathon and thought that he had to run for 26 days, not 26 miles. Reportedly, the blissfully unaware Nakajimi was somewhere out there determined to finish the race. Various people had spotted him still running, but nobody had been able to flag him down.

1986: The *Parisien* newspaper stunned its readers when it reported that the Eiffel Tower was to be dismantled and reconstructed in the new Euro Disney theme park to the east of Paris.

1995: *Discover* magazine reported that the highly respected wildlife biologist Dr Aprile Pazzo had discovered a new species in Antarctica: the hot-headed naked ice borer. This fascinating creature had a bony plate on its head which could become burning hot, allowing the animal to bore through the ice at high speeds. By this method it was able to hunt penguins, melting the ice beneath the penguins and catching them when they sank down into the slush. *Discover* received more letters in response to this article than to any other article in their history.

1997: An email message went around the world announcing that the internet would be shut down for cleaning for 24 hours from 31 March until 2 April. This cyber-cleaning was said to be essential to clear out the 'electronic flotsam and jetsam' that had accumulated in the network and was threatening to block it completely. The cleaning would be done

by five very powerful Japanese-built multi-lingual internet-crawling robots. All dead websites and emails would be purged. During this period, all users were warned to disconnect all devices from the internet. The message supposedly originated from the 'Interconnected Network Maintenance Staff, Main Branch, Massachusetts Institute of Technology'. This was an updated version of an old joke that used to be told about the telephone system. For many years, gullible phone customers had been warned that the phone systems would be cleaned on April Fool's Day. They were cautioned to place plastic bags over the ends of the phone to catch the dust that might be blown out of the phone lines during this period.

1998: The New Mexicans for Science and Reason newsletter featured an article claiming that the Alabama state legislature had voted to change the value of the mathematical constant pi from 3.14159 to the 'Biblical value' of 3.0. The article went onto the internet, and then it rapidly spread. The Alabama legislature began receiving hundreds of calls from people all over the world protesting the legislation.

2000: The *Daily Mail* announced that Esporta Health Clubs had launched an innovative new type of sock that could help people lose weight. Dubbed 'FatSox', these revolutionary socks could suck body fat out of sweaty feet.

2000: Early morning commuters driving up the northern carriageway of the M3 near Farnborough, Hampshire, encountered a pedestrian zebra crossing painted across the busy motorway. The perpetrator of the prank was unknown.

2002: Tesco published an advertisement in the *Sun* newspaper announcing the successful development of a genetically modified 'whistling carrot'. Their ad explained that the carrots had been grown with air holes in their side, which would

whistle when the vegetable was cooked.

2008: The BBC announced that staff filming near the Antarctic for its natural history series *Miracles of Evolution* had witnessed penguins flying through the air. The BBC even offered a clip of these flying penguins, which became one of the most viewed videos on the internet. A follow-up video later showed how the BBC created the special effects of the flying penguins.

2011: IKEA Australia announced their latest product as the 'IKEA Hundstol', also known as a highchair for dogs. News of the product was placed on IKEA Australia's Facebook page, complete with a link to a YouTube video where an IKEA designer discussed the safety features of the 'aesthetically pleasing' chair.

2012: Sir Richard Branson announced the launch of Virgin Volcanic, which would journey to the core of an active volcano. 'Only 500 people have been to space, only three people have been to the bottom of the ocean, but no one has ever attempted to journey to the core of an active volcano. Until now,' said Sir Richard. The following year, the billionaire announced the introduction of glass-bottomed planes: 'I'm thrilled to announce that Virgin has created another world first with the introduction of the technology required to produce the world's first glass-bottomed plane. This technological innovation coincides with

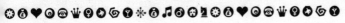

the start of Virgin Atlantic Airways' first ever domestic service to Scotland.'

2013: The video-sharing site Vimeo changed its name to Vimeow to become a site for sharing videos of your pet cat . . . but only for a day!

2013: It was announced that Tic Tac – best known for their tiny mints – would be introducing a new flavour: pizza. Try using that as a breath freshener!

French words or phrases commonly used in English

à la carte: individual food items ordered off a menu, as opposed to a set meal menu

à propos: regarding/concerning

adieu: farewell, as opposed to *au revoir,* which means 'see you later'

adroit: dexterous, clever. This comes from the French word 'droit' meaning 'right'. Compare this to *gauche* – or left – which has come to mean 'clumsy'

apéritif: a drink before a meal

au fait: to know something

au pair: a young foreigner who does domestic chores in exchange for room and board

avant-garde: cutting-edge art, music and literature

blasé: jaded

bon voyage: have a good journey

bric-à-brac: small ornamental objects

café: a coffee shop

c'est la vie!: such is life!

chauffeur: a driver

chic: stylish

cliché: a stereotype

couture: high fashion (also, *couturier:* a fashion designer)

crèche: a place where parents leave young children

crème de la crème: best of the best

déjà vu: 'already seen' – an impression of having seen or experienced something before

dossier: a file containing detailed information

en masse: all together

en route: on the way

enfant terrible: a disruptively unconventional person

ennui: boredom

fait accompli: something that has already happened and so can't be undone

grand prix: first prize – e.g. in motor racing

hors d'œuvre: starter, appetizer

idée fixe: obsession

joie de vivre: joy of living

laissez-faire: letting people get on with things

nom de plume: author's pseudonym

objet d'art: work of art

papier-mâché: craft using paper and paste

soirée: an evening party

soupçon: very small amount

tête-à-tête: private conversation between two people

volte-face: complete reversal of opinion

German words or phrases commonly used in English

abseil: drop to the ground using a rope

angst: general feeling of fear or worry

blitz: lightning fast

bratwurst: type of sausage

doppelgänger: double or lookalike

ersatz: replacement

fest: festival

flak: criticism

frankfurter: type of sausage – usually served as a hot dog

hinterland: other interests apart from your main occupation

kaput: broken

kindergarten: preschool

kitsch: cheap, sentimental, gaudy

poltergeist: alleged paranormal phenomenon where objects appear to move

pumpernickel: type of rye bread

rucksack: backpack

sauerkraut: fermented cabbage

schadenfreude: delight at the misfortune of others

strudel: pastry

wanderlust: the yearning to travel

wunderkind: child prodigy

zeitgeist: spirit of the age

Genuine things written by school students in History essays

The greatest writer of the Renaissance was William Shakespeare. He was born in the year 1564, supposedly on his birthday. He never made much money and is famous only because of his plays. Romeo and Juliet are an example of a heroic couplet.

Actually, Homer was not written by Homer but by another man of that name.

Solomon had 300 wives and 700 porcupines.

Nero was a cruel tyranny who would torture his subjects by playing the fiddle to them.

Joan of Arc was burnt to a steak and was cannonized by Bernard Shaw.

It was an age of great inventions and discoveries. Gutenberg invented removable type and the Bible. Another important invention was the circulation of blood.

Sir Walter Raleigh is a historical figure because he invented cigarettes and started smoking.

Writing at the same time as Shakespeare was Miguel Cervantes. He wrote Donkey Hote. The next great author was John Milton. Milton wrote Paradise Lost. Then his wife died and he wrote Paradise Regained.

During the Renaissance America began. Christopher Columbus was a great navigator who discovered America while cursing about the Atlantic. Later, the Pilgrims crossed the ocean, and this was called Pilgrim's Progress. The winter of 1620 was a hard one for the settlers. Many

**people died and many babies were born.
Captain John Smith was responsible for all
this.**

One of the causes of the Revolutionary War
was the English putting tacks in their tea.
Also, the colonists would send their parcels
through the post without stamps. Finally
the colonists won the war and no longer
had to pay for taxis.

**Soon the Constitution of the United States
was adopted to secure domestic hostility.
Under the constitution the people enjoyed
the right to keep bare arms.**

Meanwhile in Europe, the enlightenment
was a reasonable time. Voltaire invented
electricity and also wrote a book called
Candy. Gravity was invented by Isaac
Walton. It is chiefly noticeable in the
autumn when the apples are falling off the
trees.

**The French Revolution was accomplished
before it happened and catapulted into**

Napoleon. Napoleon wanted an heir to inherit his power, but since Josephine was a baroness, she couldn't have any children.

The countries which produce the most . . .

Artichokes – Italy

Asparagus – Spain

Avocados – Mexico

Cabbages – China

Carrots – China

Cashew Nuts – Vietnam

Cauliflowers – India

Cherries – Italy

Cork – Portugal (half the cork in the world comes from there)

Corn – The US

Currants – Russia

Dates – Iran

Eggs – China

Figs – Turkey

Grapefruits – The US

Hazelnuts – Turkey

Honey – China

Mangoes – India

Maple Syrup – Canada (more than 75 per cent of the world's supply of maple syrup comes from there)

Olives – Spain

Oranges – Brazil

Pigs – China

Pineapples – Thailand

Pistachio Nuts – Iran

Potatoes – China

Raspberries – Russia

Strawberries – The US

'Laws' named after people

Brooks' law: Adding manpower to a late software project makes it later.

Clarke's three laws:
First law: When a distinguished but elderly scientist states that something is possible, he is almost certainly right. When he states that something is impossible, he is very probably wrong.

Second law: The only way of discovering the limits of the possible is to venture a little way past them into the impossible.

Third law: Any sufficiently advanced technology is indistinguishable from magic.

Dilbert principle: The worst workers are systematically moved to the place where they can do the least damage . . . which is management.

Goodhart's law: When a measure becomes a target, it ceases to be a good measure.

Hanlon's razor: Never attribute to malice that which can be adequately explained by stupidity.

Herblock's law: If it's good, they'll stop making it.

Hofstadter's law: It always takes longer than you expect, even when you take into account Hofstadter's law.

Hutber's law: Improvement means deterioration.

Occam's razor: When two explanations

are offered for a phenomenon, the simpler explanation is preferable.

Parkinson's law: Work expands so as to fill the time available for its completion.

Peter principle: In a hierarchy, every employee tends to rise to his level of incompetence.

Roemer's law: If you build a hospital bed, it will be filled.

Rothbard's law: Everyone specializes in their own area of weakness.

Segal's law: A man with a watch knows what time it is. A man with two watches is never sure.

Skitt's law: Any post correcting an error in another post will contain at least one error itself.

Sturgeon's law: Nothing is always absolutely so.

Sturgeon's revelation: 90 per cent of everything is crud.

Sutton's law: Go where the money is (named after bank robber Willie Sutton who, when asked why he robbed banks, is claimed to have answered 'Because that's where the money is.')

Unbelievable, but true!

The three wealthiest families in the world have more assets than the combined wealth of the 48 poorest nations.

Because he felt that such an important tool should be public property, English chemist John Walker never patented his invention – matches.

More than 25 per cent of the world's forests are in Siberia.

Justin Timberlake's half-eaten French toast sold for more than £1,500 on eBay.

The largest swimming pool in the world is in the Chilean resort of San Alfonso del Mar. It's a kilometre long and 35 metres deep.

The inventor of Vaseline ate a spoonful of his invention every morning (don't try this at home!).

The longest recorded fart lasted two minutes, 42 seconds.

The Cairo Opera House was destroyed by fire in 1970. Unfortunately, the Cairo fire station was located inside the same building.

An estimated 300,000 accidents a year are caused by sat navs.

St George, the patron saint of England, never actually visited England.

The world record for skimming stones across the water is 51 skips.

An American office worker died after choking on some dried skin which he'd bitten off his own foot.

Modern hair conditioners were introduced at the turn of the last century to soften men's hair, beards and moustaches.

Mailing an entire building has been illegal in the US since 1916, when a man mailed a 40,000-ton brick house across Utah to avoid high transport costs.

In 1924 the French Boxing Federation banned boxers from kissing each other at the end of a contest.

The warmest temperature ever recorded on Antarctica was minus16 degrees Celsius.

In 1977 a 13-year-old child found a tooth growing out of his left foot.

The capital of San Marino, the city of San

Marino, isn't in fact the largest city in San Marino: Dogana is.

There are so many vehicles in Hong Kong that if they were all out driving at the same time they wouldn't fit on the roads.

Just over 100 people in Scotland own almost a third of the country's land.

The odds of seeing three albino deer at once are one in 79 billion, yet one man in Boulder Junction, Wisconsin, took a picture of three albino deer in the woods.

In medieval Japan, when men wished to seal an agreement, they urinated together, crisscrossing their streams of urine.

The longest recorded leg hair is ten centimetres long.

In Taiwan, drunk drivers are given the option of playing Mah Jong (a sort of card game played with tiles) with the elderly instead of paying a fine.

At the height of its popularity in Japan, the arcade game Space Invaders caused a nationwide coin shortage.

The ancient Egyptians bought jewellery for their pet crocodiles.

A five-and-a-half-year-old girl, who wasn't able to sweat, weighed 113 kilos. She was put on display at an exhibition in Vienna in 1894.

The men who served as guards along the Great Wall of China in the Middle Ages were often born on the wall, grew up there, married there, died there and were buried within it. Many of these guards never left the wall in their entire lives.

Van Halen had a stipulation in their concert contracts that a bowl of M&Ms be provided in their dressing room with all the brown ones removed. They once trashed a dressing room after this demand wasn't met.

The Nazi leader Hermann Goering refused to use regulation toilet paper and had to bulk-buy soft white handkerchiefs instead.

The most push-ups ever performed in one day was 46,001.

The launching mechanism of a carrier ship that helps planes to take off could throw a pick-up truck over a mile.

An ancient cure for bed-wetting was to eat fried mice.

A double-leg amputee named Bob Wieland took three years, eight months and six days to 'walk' on his hands across the US.

The former Welsh rugby union international Harry Payne played his last game of rugby after breaking his ankle in a match in 1992. He was 84 years old.

Dr John Pemberton, the man who invented Coca-Cola in 1896, sold the formula the following year for just $2,300.

The search engine Yahoo was originally called 'Jerry and David's Guide to the World Wide Web'.

In 1840 a Hudson's Bay Company fur trader fell out of a tree, which he'd climbed to get a better view of the terrain, and tore open his abdomen, but he pushed his intestines back inside, recovered and continued his journey.

Animals that are now extinct in the British Isles

Arctic fox (became extinct in the British Isles around 10,000 BC)

Arctic lemming (c. 8000 BC)

Brown bear (c. 1000 AD)

Cave lion (c. 10,000 BC)

Eurasian lynx (c. 400 AD)

Eurasian wolf (1740)

Irish elk (c. 6000 BC)

Narrow-headed vole (c. 8000 BC)

Root vole (c. 1500 BC)

Saiga antelope (c. 10,000 BC)

Wolverine (c. 6000 BC)

Woolly mammoth (c. 10,000 BC)

Woolly rhinoceros (c. 10,000 BC)

Genuine complaints received by travel companies

I think it should be explained in the brochure that the local store does not sell proper biscuits like custard creams or ginger nuts.

We booked an excursion to a water park but no one told us we had to bring our swimming costumes and towels.

We found the sand was not like the sand in the brochure. Your brochure shows the sand as yellow but it was white.

We bought 'Ray-Ban' sunglasses for five Euros (£3.50) from a street trader, only to find out they were fake.

I compared the size of our one-bedroom apartment to our friends' three-bedroom apartment and ours was significantly smaller.

The brochure stated: 'No hairdressers

at the accommodation'. We're trainee hairdressers – will we be OK staying here?

There are too many Spanish people. The receptionist speaks Spanish. The food is Spanish. Too many foreigners.

And this year we're going walking in the OFF PEAK District – it's much cheaper

We had to queue outside with no air conditioning.

It is your duty as a tour operator to advise us of noisy or unruly guests before we travel.

I was bitten by a mosquito – no one said they could bite.

It's lazy of the local shopkeepers to close in the afternoons. I often needed to buy things during 'siesta' time – this should be banned.

On my holiday to Goa in India, I was disgusted to find that almost every restaurant served curry. I don't like spicy food at all.

The beach was too sandy.

Topless sunbathing on the beach should be banned. The holiday was ruined as my husband spent all day looking at other women.

No one told us there would be fish in the sea. The children were startled.

It took us nine hours to fly home from Jamaica to England – it only took the Americans three hours to get home.

Shortest wars

Britain against Zanzibar (1896) – 38 minutes

Six-Day War (Israel against various Arab countries) (1967) – 6 days

Slovenia and Yugoslavia (1991) – 10 days

India against Pakistan (1971) – 13 days

Serbia against Bulgaria (1885) – 14 days

Georgia against Armenia (1918) – 24 days

China against Vietnam (1979) – 27 days

Greece against Turkey (1897) – 30 days

Second Balkan War (Bulgaria against Serbia and Greece) (1913) – 32 days

Poland against Lithuania (1920) – 37 days

The Falklands War (Britain against Argentina) (1982) – 42 days

Secret service codenames

POTUS: President of the United States

FLOTUS: First Lady of the United States

VPOTUS: Vice President of the United States

Eagle: Bill Clinton

Evergreen: Hillary Clinton

Renegade: Barack Obama

Renaissance: Michelle Obama

Celtic: Joe Biden

Denali: Sarah Palin

Kittyhawk: Queen Elizabeth II

Unicorn: Prince Charles

The USA

The name California was taken from a 16th-century Spanish novel, *The Exploits of Esplaidián* by García Ordóñez de Montalvo, who described it as a mythical Amazon kingdom.

At General Motors, the cost of health care for employees exceeds the cost of steel.

One out of every eight couples married in the US last year met online.

58 per cent of American men say they are happier after divorce.

85 per cent of American women say they are happier after divorce.

The United States Postal Service handles over 40 per cent of the world's mail volume.

The US has the highest number of marriages and remarriages.

The US eastern seaboard consumes almost 50 per cent of all ice-cream sandwiches.

Sometimes, the number of hot-dog sales at a baseball stadium exceeds the number of spectators – though, typically, hot-dog sales at ballparks average 80 per cent of the attendance.

Every citizen of the state of Alaska over the age of six months receives an oil dividend cheque of about $1,000 per year.

More than one million dogs and cats have been made the main beneficiaries in US wills.

The state of Oregon has one city named Sisters and another called Brothers. Sisters got its name from a nearby trio of peaks in the Cascade Mountains known as the Three Sisters. Brothers was named as a counterpart to Sisters.

The exact geographic centre of the United States is near Lebanon, Kansas.

Six per cent of American men propose marriage by phone.

An old law in Bellingham, Washington, made it illegal for a woman to take more than three steps backwards while dancing.

In Michigan, there was a law forbidding a woman to cut her own hair without her husband's permission.

The average American eats at McDonald's more than 1,800 times in their life.

There is enough water in American swimming pools to cover the whole city of San Francisco to a depth of more than two metres.

Some two million Americans are in jail at any moment in time.

At 21, the United States has the highest minimum drinking age in the world.

The United States has never lost a war when donkeys were used.

US soldiers' dried food rations can be re-hydrated with urine.

The US has more bagpipe bands than Scotland does.

When the divorce rate goes up in the

United States, toy makers say the sale of toys also rises.

There are over a million swimming pools in Florida, even though the sea is never more than 80 miles away.

There's a petrol station in the US state of Washington which is shaped like a teapot.

There are four US states where the first letter of the capital city is the same as the first letter of the state: Dover, Delaware; Honolulu, Hawaii; Indianapolis, Indiana; and Oklahoma City, Oklahoma.

Courses offered at (proper) American colleges include: Philosophy of *Star Trek*, Tree Climbing, Maple Syrup and Stupidity.

There's a microwave cookery school in the US.

There's a professional American boxer named Boyd 'Rainmaker' Melson who donates all the money he earns boxing to fund stem-cell research.

Science and nature

A hard-boiled egg will spin. An uncooked or soft-boiled egg will not.

The oil used by jewellers to lubricate clocks and watches costs about $3,000 a gallon.

The volume of the earth's moon is the same as the volume of the Pacific Ocean.

The heart of an astronaut actually gets smaller while in outer space.

Sound at the right vibration can bore holes through a solid object.

When Anders Celsius, the creator of the temperature scale that bears his name (Celsius – not Andreas), first developed his scale, he made freezing 100 degrees and boiling 0 degrees (i.e. the wrong way round). Since no one dared point this out to him, his fellow scientists waited until Celsius died to change the scale.

Airports at higher altitudes require a longer airstrip.

There is the same quantity of water on earth today as there was four billion years ago.

A man uses more energy shaving with a hand razor at a sink (because of the water power, the water pump and so on) than he would by using an electric razor.

Experiments conducted in Germany and at the University of Southampton in England show that even small noises cause the pupils of the eyes to dilate. It is believed that this is why surgeons, watchmakers and others who perform delicate manual operations are so bothered by noise. The sounds cause their pupils to change focus and blur their vision.

Lightning doesn't always produce thunder.

About 20 per cent of the earth is permanently frozen.

The setting sun is redder than the rising sun because the air at the end of the day is generally dustier than it is at the beginning.

In 1978 an experiment at Princeton University in the US generated a temperature of 70 million degrees. It remains the highest man-made temperature ever recorded.

Rocket launches, nuclear explosions and volcanic eruptions can all trigger lightning.

Because metal expands in heat, the Eiffel Tower always leans away from the sun.

There are mirrors on the moon. They were left there by astronauts who wanted to bounce laser beams off them, so that the distance to the moon could be measured.

The watermelon originated in Africa, and there's evidence of its cultivation in the Nile Valley from as early as the second millennium BC. A typical watermelon is 91.45 per cent water.

The degree sign (°) is thought to be an ancient representation of the sun.

The deepest borehole drilled in the world was 17,400 metres deep (Azerbaijan, 2002).

El Salvador's tropical vegetation includes more than 200 species of orchids.

A ball of glass will bounce higher than a ball of rubber. A ball of solid steel will bounce higher than one made entirely of glass.

Because of its varied landscape and climate, Turkey is one of the richest countries in the world in varieties of flowers, with approximately 9,000 species, of which 3,000 are native to Turkey.

Almost all of Madagascar's plants are unique to that country and can't be found anywhere else in the world. And there are also several animal species unique to the island.

The lowest temperature ever recorded in the UK is minus 27.2 degrees Celsius – on three occasions, the most recent being in 1995.

THE PHONETIC ALPHABET

Alpha – A

Bravo – B

Charlie – C

Delta – D

Echo – E

Foxtrot – F

Golf – G

Hotel – H

India – I

Juliet – J

Kilo – K

Lima – L

Mike – M

November – N

Oscar – O

Papa – P

Quebec – Q

Romeo – R

Sierra – S

Tango – T

Uniform – U

Victor – V

Whisky – W

X–Ray – X

Yankee – Y

Zulu – Z

Place names

Albania is also known as Shqiperia, which means 'Land of the Eagles'.

Haiti and the Dominican Republic share the island of Hispaniola. The Taínos (the original inhabitants) called the island

Quisqueya, meaning 'mother of the earth' or 'mother of all lands'.

Christopher Columbus landed on Dominica in 1493. As he landed on a Sunday, he called the island Dominica (Sunday).

Colombia has changed its official name several times. It has been called:

- Virreynato de la Nueva Granada
- Gran Colombia
- República de Nueva Granada
- Confederación Granadina
- Estados Unidos de Nueva Granada
- Estados Unidos de Colombia.

Tallinn means 'Danish castle' in Estonian.

The name Albania comes from Albanoi, which was the name of an Illyrian tribe in the second century BC.

St Kitts & Nevis are two Caribbean islands linked for administrative purposes. St Kitts is really St Christopher, named by – who

else? – Christopher Columbus after his patron saint. However, it is known as St Kitts for short.

Christopher Columbus also gave the island of Puerto Rico its first name – San Juan Bautista – in honour of St John the Baptist. This was shortened to San Juan. Eventually the island changed its name to Puerto Rico (the Spanish for 'Rich Port') but kept San Juan as the name of the capital. The island is also popularly known as 'La Isla del Encanto', which translates as 'The Island of Enchantment'.

In 1493 Columbus sighted Antigua from near Redonda and named it Antigua after the Church of Santa María de la Antigua in Seville.

The technical name of Greece is the Hellenic Republic.

Amman, the capital of Jordan, was called Philadelphia at one time.

The Gaelic for Ireland is Eire.

The name Australia was popularized by the navigator and mapmaker Matthew Flinders, who is believed to be the first person to circumnavigate the country. His 1814 book *A Voyage to Terra Australis,* is regarded as the first important work on Australia.

The film version of *Popeye* was filmed in Malta, and a village on the island was renamed Popeye Village.

Bahrain derives its name from an Arabic word meaning 'two seas', which refers to the blend of fresh water springs and sea water in the country.

The name of Tanzania's largest city, Dar es Salaam, means 'Haven of Peace'.

The name Canada literally means 'village'. It comes from the St Lawrence Iroquoian word *kanata*, meaning village or settlement. When the French explorer Jacques Cartier travelled up the St Lawrence River in 1534, he asked the

indigenous peoples what they called their land. Not unreasonably, they answered 'Kanata'. Cartier took their answer to mean the whole country and so he put that on his map.

Barbados was first recorded with the spelling Barbadoes.

There's an island off the coast of Tanzania called Mafia.

Mammals, birds and insects and the sounds they make

Alligators – bellow, hiss

Apes – gibber

Badgers – growl

Bats – screech

Bears – growl

Bees – hum and buzz

Beetles – drone

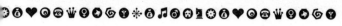

Bulls – bellow

Camels – grunt

Cats – purr, miaow and hiss

Chickens – cluck

Cocks – crow

Cows – moo

Coyotes – yelp, cry

Crickets – chirp

Cuckoos – coo, cuckoo

Dogs – bark, woof

Dolphins – click

Donkeys – bray, hee-haw

Doves – coo

Ducks – quack

Eagles – scream, cry

Elephants – trumpet

Frogs – croak, ribbet

Goats – bleat

Geese – cackle, honk, quack

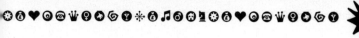

Hamsters – squeak

Hippopotamuses – bellow, rumble, roar, growl

Hogs – grunt

Horses – neigh, snort, whinny

Hyenas – laugh

Jackals – howl

Lambs – bleat

Lions – roar

Llamas – growl

Magpies – chatter

Mice – squeak

Monkeys – chatter, gibber

Nightingales – sing, warble

Owls – hoot

Parrots – talk, screech, squawk

Penguins – honk

Pigs – oink, snort, grunt, squeal

Pigeons – coo

Rabbits – squeak, drum

Rats – squeak

Rhinos – bellow

Seagulls – scream

Sheep – bleat, baa

Snakes – hiss

Stags – bellow

Tigers – growl, roar

Tortoises – Grunt

Turkeys – gobble

Vultures – scream

Walruses – groan

Whales – sing

Wolves – howl

Zebras – neigh, whinny

English (well, almost) as it is written around the world (2)

In an Acapulco hotel:
The manager has personally passed all the water served here

Sign in an American hospital:
guard dogs operating

Sign outside a Mexican disco:
members and non-members only

Sign in an American draper's shop:
gents' trousers slashed

On a string of Chinese-made Christmas lights:
for indoor or outdoor use only

From a Japanese information booklet about using a hotel air conditioner:
cooles and heates: if you want just condition of warm in your room, please control yourself

Found on an American butane lighter:
warning: flame may cause fire

From a brochure of a car rental firm in Tokyo:
when passenger of foot heave in sight, tootle the horn. trumpet him melodiously at first, but if he still obstacles your passage then tootle him with vigor

Detour sign in Kyushi, Japan:
stop – drive sideways

Advertisement for donkey rides in Thailand:
would you like to ride on your own ass?

Sign outside a Bangkok bar:
the shadiest cocktail bar in town

Sign in a Sri Lankan swimming pool:
*do not use the diving board when the
swimming pool is empty*

Outside a Hong Kong tailor shop:
ladies may have a fit upstairs

German – English textbook:
*after a certain time cheques are stale and
cannot be cashed*

Sign in a travel agent's in Barcelona:
go away!

Sign in a French swimming pool:
*swimming forbidden in the absence of a
saviour*

From a restaurant in France:
*a sports jacket may be worn to dinner, but
no trousers*

Sign in a hotel in Ankara:
*please hang your order before retiring on
your doorknob*

In a Copenhagen airline ticket office:
*we take your bags and send them in all
directions*

Sign in a British hospital:
*dangerous drugs must be locked up with
the matron*

On the door of a Moscow hotel room:
*if this is your first visit to the ussr, you are
welcome to it*

In a Belgrade hotel lift:
*to move the cabin, push button for wishing
floor. if the cabin should enter more
persons, each one should press a number
of wishing floor. driving is then going*

alphabetically by national order

In a Norwegian cocktail lounge:
ladies are requested not to have children in the bar

From Budapest:
all rooms not denounced by twelve o'clock will be paid for twicely

On the menu of a Swiss restaurant:
our wines leave you nothing to hope for

Sign on lion cage at a Czech zoo:
no smoothen the lion

In a Bucharest hotel lobby:
the lift is being fixed for the next day. during that time we regret that you will be unbearable

In a Balkan hotel:
the flattening of underwear with pleasure is the job of the chambermaid

In a British community centre:

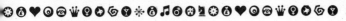

*visitors with reading difficulties should
proceed to front desk for information*

From a restaurant in Vienna:
*fried milk, children sandwiches, roast cattle
and boiled sheep*

Sign in an Istanbul hotel:
*to call room service, please open the door
and call room service*

Rhodes tailor shop:
order your summer suit. because is big rush, we will execute customers in strict rotation

In the window of a Swedish furrier:
fur coats made for ladies from their own skin

Sign in a greengrocer's:
please don't handle the fruit. ask for debbie

Sign on a building site:
night watchman patrols this area 24 hours a day

Directions for mosquito repellent:
replacing battery – replace the old battery with a new one

Sign in a hotel:
all fire extinguishers must be examined at least ten days before any fire

It's a surprising world!

Almost 90 per cent of Uruguayans are of European descent.

Lake Balkash in eastern Kazakhstan contains two kinds of water: salt water in the east and fresh water in the west.

There is nowhere in Tuvalu that's more than five metres above sea level. So if sea levels rise, the islands of Tuvalu will disappear.

Nine out of ten New York taxi drivers were born outside the US.

In Sudan, the children who live in cities celebrate their birthday whereas the children who live in the countryside don't. So where would you choose to live?

There's an Argentinian town where horses have to wear a hat if it's too hot.

In Japan some restaurants serve smaller portions to women, even though they

charge as much as they do for men's portions.

The world's largest Chinatown is in Bangkok, Thailand.

Finland has only been an independent country since 1918. Before that, it belonged to Sweden or Russia.

Brunei is separated into two parts – with Malaysia in the middle – that don't border each other.

There are over 20 kilometres of underground passages in Luxembourg.

About 60 per cent of Africa's electricity is generated in South Africa.

There are 300 times as many sheep as there are people in the Falkland Islands.

In Ancient Peru, if a woman found an odd-looking potato, she had to push it into the face of the nearest man.

The Dogon people of Mali believe that

sound and smell are very similar because they both travel through air.

The cuckoo clock originated in Germany – not Switzerland.

Montenegro has separate emergency numbers for the police and the ambulance service.

At the turn of the 19th century, Azerbaijan was producing half of all the world's oil.

There are more pyramids in Peru than there are in Egypt.

Although Mali is currently one of the world's least developed countries – almost three-quarters of its people earn less than a pound a day – there was a time when it was very wealthy.

Until 1965, Singapore was part of Malaysia.

Peru is the home of the Uros Islands. These are man-made islands created from tortora reeds.

Cyprus is geographically in Western Asia (or the Near East), though politically and culturally it is considered as being in Europe.

Slavery wasn't abolished in Mauritania until as late as 1980. And even since abolition, there have been instances of slavery.

From 1990 to 2000 Alberto Fujimori was President of Peru, even though he had dual nationality with Japan (both his parents were Japanese).

The capital of the Maldives is 'Male' – but it's not pronounced like that!

The Austrian Alps take up 62 per cent of Austria's total land mass.

There was once a bridge between Malta and Sicily.

In the Middle Ages, Lithuania was the biggest country in Europe.

There's only 5.54 centimetres of coastline per person in the world.

Pitcairn is the second largest of all the Pitcairn Islands, but it's the only one that's inhabited.

Despite its location in the heart of the

Pacific Ocean, the inhabitants of the Cook Islands are descended from Asians.

There are no permanent rivers or lakes in Malta.

The capital of Taiwan, Taipei, is built in a big flat basin that used to be a lake.

Slavery was still legal in Niger until May 2004 – and even after its abolition, it still continues without much hindrance.

South Africa has three capitals: Pretoria is the administrative capital, Cape Town is the legislative capital, and Bloemfontein is the home of the judiciary.

None of the snakes in Madagascar are poisonous.

In the United Arab Emirates, the containers used to store oil are called khazzans – each of which holds 75 million litres of oil and is big enough to cover a 15-storey building. Incidentally, the word *khazzan* means 'to store' in Arabic.

There's a Starbucks in South Korea that has five levels.

In Hungary, hot springs are used for central heating in homes.

There's a lake in Palau called Jellyfish Lake. The jellyfish in this lake rarely sting – and when they do, their sting is not very harmful to people.

Wallis and Futuna are two island groups separated by 150 miles of ocean in the central South Pacific. Since 1959 they have been joined together as a French overseas territory.

There are over 400 islands in Denmark. Less than a quarter of them are lived on.

Almost 12 per cent of the inhabitants of Luxembourg and three per cent of the people in France are of Portuguese descent.

There are places in Africa where the men (rather than the women) wear veils over their faces.

In ancient Japan, public contests were held to see who could break wind loudest and longest. Winners were awarded prizes.

There's an elephant orphanage in Sri Lanka.

There is a bathroom in Egypt where it's free to use the toilet, but you have to bring or buy your own toilet paper.

There was once an undersea post office in the Bahamas.

A man in Yemen was once found to have four kidneys.

In Bolivia, the voting age is 18 for married citizens but 21 for single people. Who knows what happens if you're aged between 18 and 20 and your wedding day is the same day as the election?

Fireworks

Remember, remember
The fifth of November,
Gunpowder, treason and plot;
I see no reason
Why gunpowder treason
Should ever be forgot.

Every fifth of November we celebrate the capture of Guy Fawkes, who attempted to blow up the Houses of Parliament

in 1605. He was tortured, hanged and then (while still alive) cut down. He was disembowelled, decapitated and then his body was cut in quarters. Just to make sure.

Penny for the Guy,
Hit him in the eye,
Stick him up a lamp-post
And there let him die.

In Lewes, East Sussex, they take Guy Fawkes Night very seriously indeed. There are five bonfire societies and they organize parades through the streets of the town, culminating in a mile-long procession of 10,000 people carrying blazing torches.

The Victorians introduced the use of fireworks to celebrate the foiling of the Gunpowder Plot.

In 1990 a family went to a public firework display because they thought setting fireworks off in their own garden was too dangerous. When they got home, they found their house had been set on fire by a neighbour's rocket, which had shattered a bedroom window.

One place where they don't let off any fireworks is St Peter's School in York. Guy Fawkes was a pupil there and they don't think it's nice to burn their old boys.

Roller coasters

The world's fastest roller coaster is the Formula Rossa, which is at Ferrari World in Abu Dhabi, the United Arab Emirates. Launched in 2010, it has a top speed of 240 kilometres per hour (150 miles per hour), which it reaches in under five seconds. To get that fast, it uses a hydraulic launch system similar to aircraft-carrier steam catapults. The roller coaster's track is 2.2 kilometres (1.4 miles) long, making it the fourth biggest in the world, behind Steel Dragon 2000 in Japan, The Ultimate

in Ripon, North Yorkshire, and The Beast in Ohio. The latter is a wooden roller coaster and the longest roller coaster in America – and the longest wooden roller coaster in the world. It sprawls over 35 acres (14 hectares).

Formula Rossa's shape was inspired by the legendary Italian racetrack of Monza. All riders are required to wear protective glasses similar to those used during skydiving because at high air-speeds riders risk being hit in the eye by insects.

While the basic concept of the roller coaster dates back to the Russian ice slides of the 1700s, the first one in which the train was attached to the track dates back to 1817 and the French Russes á Belleville (Russian Mountains of Belleville).

Food and drink

Allspice – which tastes like a combination of cinnamon, cloves, nutmeg and pepper – is, in fact, ground from the seeds of a single plant: the Jamaican pimento.

The British eat more cans of baked beans than the rest of the world combined.

Cinnamon originated in Sri Lanka.

Chocolate chip cookies were first made by mistake when the chocolate in the biscuit didn't melt properly.

90 per cent of the Vitamin C in Brussels sprouts is lost during cooking.

Goat's milk is used more widely throughout the world than cow's milk.

According to a study at Harvard University, regular coffee drinkers have about one third fewer asthma symptoms than non coffee drinkers.

All M&Ms taste the same – whatever their colour.

There are more than 2,000 different types of cheese in the world.

The powder on chewing gum is finely ground marble.

***The Journal of Consumer Research* reports that, contrary to what you might expect, healthy choice options on a menu**

actually make people more likely to order unhealthy foods. The presence of healthier options seems to make people believe their meal will be healthy too – even if they pick something unhealthy!

There are 300 distinctly different types of honey.

Sushi is actually named after the rice used to make it. The Japanese term for raw fish is 'sashimi'.

In the US, 12 per cent of Coca-Cola is consumed with or for breakfast.

Women are twice as likely as men to be vegetarians.

It takes ten kilograms of milk to make one kilogram of cheese.

Just 25 bottles of Coca-Cola were sold in its first year (1886).

After the decaffeinating process, processing companies no longer throw the caffeine

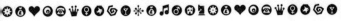

away but sell it to pharmaceutical companies.

There are two million different combinations of sandwich that can be created from a Subway menu.

'Colonial goose' is the name Australians gave to stuffed mutton.

The koran fish is found in only two places in the world: Russia and Albania. It is said to be similar to trout or carp, with a delicate flavour.

Mauritians call tomatoes 'pommes d'amour' (love apples). Mauritian tomatoes are smaller and more strongly flavoured.

Pepsi-Cola was originally called 'Brad's Drink'. It had been invented in 1893 by Caleb Bradham, who was known to the customers at his drugstore as Brad.

In Haiti, where one in five people is chronically malnourished, there's so little soil in which to grow proper food that many poor people eat 'cakes' made from clay, flavoured with salt.

Turkey has about 60 companies that manufacture chewing gum.

The Chinese started making alcohol over 3,400 years ago – 2,000 years before they first started drinking tea.

There are about 8,500 Indian restaurants in the UK.

There are over 800 different varieties of beer brewed in Belgium.

The names of countries and their origins

Countries were often named after the people who discovered and mapped them, or after the people who were found to be living there already. Sometimes countries are named after heroes or after a distinguishing feature of the landscape – like a river.

Algeria: 'The islands'
Australia: Latin for 'southern (land)'
Austria: Latin for 'eastern (land)'
Belgium: Celtic for 'brave, warlike'

Bermuda: named after Juan de Bermudez, who discovered the islands in 1503

Brazil: 'heat'

Cameroon: Portuguese for 'prawns' which were seen in the River Cameroon

Chile: 'cold, winter'

China: named after the Ch'in dynasty

Colombia: named after Christopher Columbus

Cyprus: named after copper, of which it had loads

Dominica: 'Sunday'

El Salvador: 'The saviour'

England: named after the 'Angles', who came from Germany

Eritrea: 'red', from the Greek word erythrea

The Faroe Islands: Danish for 'sheep'

France: named after the Franks, a Germanic tribe that invaded the country more than a thousand years ago

Haiti: 'mountainous'

Honduras: 'deep waters'

Hong Kong: 'fragrant harbour'

India: named after the River Indus

Indonesia: 'India', plus the Greek word for 'island'

Iran: 'worthy'

Iraq: 'lowland'

Italy: named after the Vitali tribe

Japan: the Chinese word for 'the land of the rising sun'

Korea: 'morning calm'

Kuwait: 'fort'

Lebanon: 'white mountain'

Madeira: named after the Portuguese word for 'wood' because it was heavily forested

Malawi: 'flames'

Malta: 'refuge' or 'shelter'

Mexico: 'moon water'

Mongolia: 'brave ones'

Montenegro: 'black mountain'

Morocco: 'the western kingdom'

Pakistan: derives its name from all the districts in the region: Punjab, Afghania, Kashmir, Islamabad, Sindh, and Baluchistan

Panama: 'place of many fish'

Philippines: named after King Philip II of Spain

Poland: 'land of fields'
Portugal: Latin for 'warm harbour'
Sierra Leone: 'lion-like mountains'
Singapore: Sanskrit for 'lion town' (which is curious, as there are no lions in Singapore)
Spain: 'the land of rabbits'
Thailand: 'country of the free'
Tonga: 'south' in Polynesian
Trinidad: 'Trinity' (as in the Holy Trinity)
Turkey: 'strong owner'
Uruguay: 'the river of shellfish'
Venezuela: 'Little Venice' (the houses built on stilts over the water made it look like Venice)
Vietnam: 'land of the south'
Wales: 'foreigners'
Yemen: named after the Arabic for 'right' – i.e. it's on one's right, when facing Mecca
Zimbabwe: 'houses of stone'

The underground

Today, more than 160 cities worldwide have some sort of underground rapid transit

system, with another 25 cities in different stages of building new ones.

London boasts the world's first underground railway system. It started in 1863.

The world's second underground system was Boston's, which opened in 1897.

Paris opened its Metro in 1900.

New York's subway opened in 1904 – although above-ground journeys had been made for many years before this. Indeed, some two-fifths of New York's subway is above ground.

Tokyo opened its first subway in 1927; it was to become the world's busiest.

Moscow opened its Metro in 1935. Its stations are extraordinary: some of them even have chandeliers. No wonder the system carries over 3.18 billion passengers a year.

The Los Angeles underground system wasn't fully opened until 1993, making it one of the last major cities to have a rapid transit system. But then, LA has always been the city of the car

History

As a result of King Edward VIII's abdication, the year 1936 saw three different kings on the throne: his father, George V, himself and his brother, George VI. There are two other years when this has happened: 1066 (Edward the Confessor, Harold and William the Conqueror) and 1483 (Edward IV, Edward V and Richard III).

The Persian army of 2,500 years ago used live cats as shields on the front line when fighting the Egyptians. Why? Because the Egyptians revered cats and were forbidden by law to kill them, under penalty of death.

King James VI banned the use of the surname MacGregor because the MacGregor Clan (or Clan Gregor, as it was also known) were so unruly that they caused a lot of trouble for the authorities!

During a typical medieval siege, missiles thrown by catapults occasionally included rotten food, dead horses and even captured soldiers.

Russian Tsarina Elizabeth, who ruled from 1741 to 1762, never wore a dress twice and left 15,000 dresses in her wardrobe when she died.

The Pacific Ocean was so-named by Ferdinand Magellan because it was calmer (more pacific) than the Atlantic.

The Aztec Indians of Mexico believed turquoise would protect them from physical harm, and so warriors used these green-and-blue stones to decorate their battle shields.

The earliest industrial dispute ever recorded was in 1160 BC. Workers building the tomb of Pharaoh Ramses III went on strike for higher wages.

During the American Civil War, the Vatican was the only political entity to grant official recognition to the Confederate States of America.

Archduke Karl Ludwig, brother of the Austrian emperor, was a man of such piety

that on a trip to the Holy Land in 1896, he insisted on drinking from the River Jordan, despite warnings that it would make him fatally ill. He died within a few weeks.

The Ancient Egyptians recommended mixing half an onion with beer foam as a way of warding off death.

The shoelace was invented in England in 1790. Prior to this time, all shoes were fastened with buckles.

US Civil War General Stonewall Jackson died when he was accidentally shot by one of his own men.

The Romans defeated Hannibal's elephants after they found that the elephants were afraid of the smell of horse blood. On the battlefield they slit the throats of their own horses in order to cause the enemy's mounts to panic.

Spiral staircases in medieval castles ran clockwise because all knights used to be right-handed, and so when an attacking army climbed the stairs they weren't able to use their right hands – which held the swords. Left-handed men would have had no problem, but they weren't allowed to become knights as it was assumed that they were descendants of the devil.

In the late 18th century, Poland was the

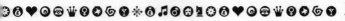
second biggest country in Europe (after Russia).

Christopher Columbus managed to avoid a battle against the people of Jamaica by convincing them he was a god. He 'predicted' the lunar eclipse of 29 February 1504, which he had read about in his almanac.

King George I (1714 – 27) was German and couldn't speak any English at the start of his reign.

During Sweden's great expansion in the 17th century, the country founded a short-lived colony in what is now Delaware in the US.

Tunisia is the region that was once known as Carthage and there was a series of wars between Carthage and Rome between 264 and 146 BC. These wars were known as the Punic Wars, and interestingly, they were only officially declared over as recently as 1985.

The British handed Suriname over to the Dutch in return for New Amsterdam – which they renamed New York.

Between the two world wars, France had 40 different governments.

As late as 1876 there were over a million slaves in Brazil. This amounted to 15 per cent of the Brazilian population.

The Swiss Guard is the world's oldest army. The earliest detachment was in 1497, and the Papal Swiss Guard in the Vatican (established in 1506) still exists today. The uniform worn by the Swiss Guard was designed by Michelangelo.

Pitcairn Island was settled in 1790 by British mutineers from the ship *Bounty*, led by Fletcher Christian, who had mutinied against the captain, William Bligh.

King Philip II of Spain had a palace with 2,673 doors.

The capital city of Morocco has changed several times during its history. Under the Romans, it was Tangier. Marrakesh was the capital between the 11th and 13th centuries, and again briefly in the 16th century. Fez was the capital from the 13th century to 1912, when the capital was changed to Rabat.

France and England fought for 150 years over the Caribbean island of Anguilla.

Juan Perón was President of Argentina twice: 1946 – 55 and 1973 – 74. After he died, his tomb was vandalized and his hands were stolen.

In 1661 Bombay (then seven islands) was given by the Portuguese to King Charles II of England in a dowry for his marriage to Catherine of Braganza. It was then leased to the British East India Company in 1668 for £10 a year! Today, Bombay (or Mumbai, as it is now known) is the financial capital of India.

Ethiopia was one of the few African countries not to be fully colonized. This is why the late Emperor Haile Selassie was worshipped as a god by Rastafarians. Having said that, it was briefly occupied by Italy in the 1930s.

In Rwanda, the mwami (king) was considered a sacred being whose power was of divine origin. The mwami had a drum that was too holy to be used, but was a symbol of his authority. Rwanda became a republic in 1961, but its last king – Kigeli V – continued to maintain his claim to the throne.

When a young Horatio Nelson was stationed in Antigua in the 1780s, he tried to stop them trading with the newly formed US. The Antiguans depended on this trade so Nelson was terribly unpopular on the island.

Zimbabwe was a mighty empire in the Middle Ages.

During the Great Fire of London, the diarist Samuel Pepys buried his precious cheese in the garden to try to save it from the flames.

Hey! can't you do this more CAERPHILLY?

King Henry VIII suffered from scurvy because, in the 16th century, wealthy people ate meat while vegetables were for peasants.

When he was 25, Julius Caesar was captured by pirates. After he was ransomed, he pursued them, captured them and had them crucified.

In 1942 the Canadians staged a simulated Nazi invasion of Winnipeg. There was one report of bloodshed – from a woman who cut her thumb while preparing toast.

During the Second World War, 27 US Marines threw themselves onto exploding grenades to save their comrades. Only three of these 27 heroes survived.

The inventor Thomas Edison claimed that he didn't need to sleep. However, he had a camp bed next to his laboratory and took enough naps to make regular sleep unnecessary.

The ancient Chinese invented the compass, the wheelbarrow and the speedometer.

In 532 AD the Byzantine Empire and Sassanid Persia concluded the Eternal Peace treaty. The peace lasted just eight years.

In Kent, in the eighth century AD, a slave forced to work on the Sabbath was entitled to be granted his freedom.

The earliest known English patent for an invention was granted by King Henry VI to Flemish-born John of Utynam in 1449. The patent gave him a 20-year monopoly for a previously unknown method of making stained glass which was required for the windows of Eton College.

Customs and traditions from around the world

A wedding feast in Yemen lasts for up to 21 days.

Filipino children will often take the hand of an elder and place it on their forehead as a sign of respect.

On New Year's Eve in Spain, people eat grapes as the clock strikes midnight.

Twelve grapes symbolize good luck for each month of the New Year.

Eritreans will commonly scoop up food and put it in the mouth of a loved one or guest. The act is a sign of affection.

Peruvians will offer you an item enthusiastically if you admire it and might be offended if you don't accept it.

Korean women cover their mouths while laughing.

In many homes in Nigeria, people clean their teeth using chewing sticks.

In the marriage ceremony of the ancient Inca Indians of Peru, the couple was only considered properly wed when they took off their sandals and handed them to each other.

Some Bolivians bring their new cars to the shrine of the Virgin of Candelaria to have them blessed. A local priest blesses the car, and then the owner showers it with champagne.

The Onge of the Andaman Islands don't ask 'How are you?' but 'How is your nose?' The correct response is to say you are 'heavy with odour'.

In Denmark, when it's a child's birthday, they fly a flag out of a window so that everyone knows.

In Bosnia and Herzegovina, it's considered impolite to beckon with the index finger or to shout in public.

Most Thais believe that people are only incidental (that's to say unimportant) occupants of land and property, which rightfully belong to local guardian spirits. Most homes have a spirit house in the garden, some of which are miniature replicas of the main house, set on a pole. Incense, flowers and food are offered to the spirits every day.

Cloth is highly valued in Bhutan, and is a traditional gift at funerals and other occasions. It is given in uneven numbers for superstitious reasons, and the amount indicates the status of the giver. Money in an envelope may be used as a substitute, along with a white scarf – the giving of which is a must for the Bhutanese at important events. The receiver of the gift mustn't open it until they are alone – to do otherwise would be bad manners and

imply that they wanted another gift. Gifts between equals are always reciprocated. However, when a gift is of significant value and comes from a person of high status, it is reciprocated with loyalty and service rather than another gift.

Argentinians celebrate a Day of Friendship every year at the end of June.

In ancient Egypt, the High Priest was the only person allowed to wear cotton.

Traditionally, an Albanian bride gave her mother-in-law a carpet woven either by her mother or herself.

During Christmas Eve dinner in Slovakia, people save food for carol-singers and visitors. In the old days, Slovakian peasants used to take a little of each Christmas dish and give it to the domestic animals.

In Denmark, to 'smash' in the New Year, young people bang on friends' doors at midnight.

In Singapore, 40 days after its birth, a baby is dressed in the lucky colour red and shown off to relatives.

In Swaziland, girls and boys have their ears pierced and keep bits of straw in the holes because they don't have earrings.

The way we live

A person is likely to eat twice as much in the company of others as when eating alone.

The average British woman's handbag contains £550 worth of possessions.

The British drink about 75 million cups of coffee a day.

The average British person eats 2.8 unhealthy snacks a day.

According to restaurant staff, married men tip better than unmarried men.

Most people who read the word 'yawning' will yawn themselves soon afterwards.

The British use almost twice as much soap as the French do.

Only about six per cent of women fail to cry at least once a month, while 50 per cent of men fail to cry that often.

The busiest time for 999 calls is between 10.30 p.m. and midnight (around 6,000 calls per hour).

78 people die each year playing Twister.

The average person speaks almost 5,000 words a day – although almost 80 per cent of speaking is self-talk (talking to yourself).

Almost two thirds of British people choose a shower rather than a bath.

The average single man is one inch shorter than the average married man.

Kids' stuff

When Microsoft founder Bill Gates was at school, he was so clever that the school paid him to draw up the school's timetable. He ensured that he was put in classes that were mostly female. When he was just 15, he designed a traffic-control system for the city of Seattle.

In 1928 the Italian gymnast Luigina Giavotti became the youngest Olympic medallist of all time, when she helped the Italian gymnastics team to win a silver medal. She was just 11 years old at the time!

Eight years later, the Danish swimmer Inge Sorensen won a bronze medal in the 200 metres breaststroke at the age of just 12, making her the youngest ever medallist in an individual event.

About ten per cent of the workforce in Egypt is under 12 years of age. Although there are laws protecting children, they're not well enforced – partly because many poverty-stricken parents need to send their children out to help support the family.

The youngest published author is Dorothy Straight of Virginia, USA who wrote *How the World Began* (Pantheon, 1964) when she was just four years old.

The youngest pope was Benedict IX (1045), who was 12 years old.

Sports

In a 1958 cricket Test against New Zealand, England's innings was opened by an international rugby union player and an international soccer player. Let me explain: the cricketer Arthur Milton also represented England at soccer, while his

opening partner, Mike Smith, won a rugby union cap for England.

Everton, Arsenal and Crystal Palace have all had trawlers named after them.

There have been archaeological finds to suggest that the Chinese engaged in sporting activities as early as 4000 BC.

In 1924 Paavo Nurmi of Finland won five gold medals. Two of these were in the 1,500 metres and 5,000 metres, in the space of just one hour. In fact, he had just

26 minutes rest between the end of the first final and the beginning of the next.

Prior to the 1987 Rugby World Cup, the United States was technically the reigning international champion, having taken the gold medal at the 1924 Summer Olympics rugby tournament.

According to research, four out of every five professional boxers have sustained brain damage.

Bowlers dream of getting hat-tricks – especially in Test matches – so you can imagine how excited Chris Tremlett was when he made his debut for England (against Bangladesh in 2005) and took two wickets in two balls. On his hat-trick ball, Mohammad Ashraful defended the ball which bounced on the ground and landed on the stumps, but because the bails did not come off, Tremlett was denied a hat-trick.

A microwaved baseball will fly farther than a frozen baseball.

The Australian batsman Sir Donald Bradman is without doubt the greatest batsman of all time. In his last Test innings (against England at the Oval in 1948) he needed just four runs to retire with a Test career batting average of precisely 100. To put this into context, an average of over 50 is the mark of a great player, and over 60 is almost unheard of. That's how far ahead of other batsmen 'The Don' was. But incredibly, he was bowled out on the second ball by Eric Hollies without scoring a single run. This left him with a Test average of 99.94 – at least 35 higher than his nearest competitor.

A badminton shuttlecock travels at a speed of over 110 miles per hour.

Tennis balls feature in William Shakespeare's *Henry V*.

Fishing is the world's biggest participation sport. There are about four million anglers in Britain. Football (soccer) is the world's biggest spectator sport.

The great writer Rudyard Kipling attributed Britain's failure to win the Boer War to 'Britain's obsession with sport'.

The Irishman St Leger Goold was runner-up in the 1879 Wimbledon Men's Singles Championship. In 1907 he was convicted of a brutal murder and sent to the notorious Devil's Island penal colony off French Guiana, where he died two years later.

John Landy is one of the greatest Australian runners of all time, with countless victories and records to his name. But it wasn't just his talent that endeared him to athletics fans all over the world. In the 1,500 metres final at the 1956 Australian National Championships – just before the 1956 Olympic Games, which were held in his home city of Melbourne – Landy was running the third lap when he noticed that fellow Aussie runner Ron Clarke had fallen over. Landy stopped running to help Clarke stand up and get back into the race. Incredibly,

in the final lap, Landy made up a huge deficit to win the race. According to the National Centre for History and Education in Australia, 'It was a spontaneous gesture of sportsmanship and it has never been forgotten.' A bronze sculpture capturing the moment Landy helped Clarke to his feet can be seen outside the Olympic Park in Melbourne. The much-loved Landy went on to become Governor of Victoria (the state of which Melbourne is the capital).

Burmese boxing is a violent sport in which the victor is the first one to draw blood.

Dr W. G. Grace was cricket's first superstar. Even though his career started in the 19th century, he is still remembered today as one of the great stars of the game. However, he wasn't above a little 'gamesmanship'. In particular, he would intimidate umpires – even telling one who had the temerity to give him out, 'They have come to see me bat, not to see this fellow bowl.' There's also the story of the bowler who, having finally dismissed him, asked, 'Doc, why are you going? There is still one stump standing'.

For hundreds of years, entire villages used to compete against other villages in rough, and sometimes violent, games of football.

Volleyball was invented by William Morgan of Holyoke, Massachusetts, in 1895.

Five batsmen have been left stranded on 99 not out in a Test match. Four of them had either already made Test centuries or would go on to do so, but it turned out to be the England cricketer Alex Tudor's highest Test score.

Around the world (2)

Although Somalia is named after its people, Somalis also live in many neighbouring countries due to the partitioning of eastern Africa by colonial powers.

In Jordan, they practise the craft of packing coloured sand into bottles. Each layer is carefully added to make geometric or floral designs, and tiny funnels and brushes are used to place the grains of sand precisely. When it's finished, a cork is put into the bottle to lock the design in place.

Indonesia is known as 'the Emerald of the Equator' because 45 per cent of the country is covered by forests.

As well as their given names, many Somalis also have a nickname based on their time of birth, where they come in the family or even on their appearance.

Tristan da Cunha's wonderfully named capital, Edinburgh of the Seven Seas, is often nicknamed 'The Settlement'.

In Sweden, Näver is a traditional craft that involves drying and weaving strips of the soft inner bark from a birch tree. This is then used to make bags and backpacks.

El Salvador honours its teachers on Teachers' Day (22 June), a national holiday. During the civil war, many teachers were persecuted and killed just for being members of a trade union.

There isn't a single person living in Iceland whose ancestors didn't come from another country.

In Switzerland, every citizen is legally required to have access to a bomb shelter.

Strikes and trade unions are illegal in the United Arab Emirates.

Workers at the Matsushita Electric Industrial Co. Ltd. in Japan beat dummies of their foremen with bamboo sticks to let off steam.

In Irian Jaya there's a tribe of people who use parrots to warn against intruders.

In the mountains of Albania an announcement of a birth, death or marriage is passed from one house to another by a gunshot or a shout that echoes through the mountains.

In 2006 the retired aircraft carrier USS *Oriskany* was sunk to the bottom of the Gulf of Mexico to create the world's largest artificial reef and diving centre.

Bulgarians consume more yogurt than any other people in the world.

Libya has many important Roman archaeological sites – including wells that still provide water.

Mexico City lies in the crater of a supervolcano.

Tattooing was very important in Samoa and there were ceremonies devoted to it. Tattoos were applied using the jagged teeth of combs. The comb would be dipped in ink and then etched into the man's arm.

In the jungles of South America a tribe was once discovered who had forgotten how to make fire and so carefully guarded their piles of continually burning embers. If all the fires had gone out, they would have been doomed to life without fire.

An earthquake in 2009 moved the southern tip of New Zealand 30 cm closer to Australia.

The lowest place on earth is around the Dead Sea, where it's 400 metres below sea level.

The Maldives is the world's lowest country. It's also the flattest country, with the highest point only reaching 2.5 metres. The country

would disappear completely if (or when) sea levels rise. However, the deepest point on our planet is Challenger Deep in the Mariana Trench, which is a staggering 11,033 metres below sea level.

Relative values

The King Fahd International Airport in Saudi Arabia is larger than the country of Bahrain.

Pago Pago, the capital of American Samoa, is actually just a village, but because it has the only proper harbour on the islands, it became the capital.

Belgium is the same size as the US state of Maryland.

Canada and Grenada both became British colonies in the same year – 1763.

Bangladesh is smaller than the US state of Iowa.

Canada is bigger than the United States.

Alaska has almost twice as many caribou as people.

Paris has more dogs than people.

Russia is 70 times larger than the whole of

the UK. Australia is 31 times bigger, and France is twice as big.

The UK is eight times bigger than Belgium and over 100,000 times bigger than Monaco.

The American secret service – the Central Intelligence Agency (CIA) – has its own take on the relative size of countries. Here are some examples:

Albania – 'slightly smaller than Maryland'

Austria – 'slightly smaller than Maine'

Bulgaria – 'slightly larger than Tennessee'

Chile – 'slightly smaller than twice the size of Montana'

France – 'slightly less than the size of Texas'

Germany – 'slightly smaller than Montana'

Gibraltar – 'more than ten times the size of the National Mall in Washington, DC'

Greece – 'slightly smaller than Alabama'

Hungary 'slightly smaller than Indiana'

Ireland – 'slightly larger than West Virginia'

Israel – 'slightly larger than New Jersey'

Italy – 'slightly larger than Arizona'

Monaco – 'about three times the size of the Mall in Washington, DC'

New Zealand – 'about the size of Colorado'

Saudi Arabia – 'slightly more than one-fifth the size of the US'

Mosts

Oslo is the most expensive city in the world.

The most widely cultivated fruit in the world is the apple. The second is the pear.

With two thirds men to one third women,

Qatar has the highest proportion of men to women.

Mauritius is the most densely populated country in Africa, with 610 people per square kilometre.

Luxembourg has the highest number of mobile phones per person in the world.

Indonesia has the most highly populated islands in the world, with over 239 million people living on them.

Israel has more museums per person than any other country

The Labrador retriever is Britain's most popular breed of dog.

The Netherlands has the most vehicles per square kilometre.

The most common elements in the earth's crust are oxygen, silicon and iron, in that order.

Belgium produces the greatest variety of bricks.

The most common elements in the universe are hydrogen and helium.

Mexico City has more taxis than any other city in the world.

India has the most post offices.

Relative to its population, Canada grants citizenship to more people than any other country in the world.

China has the most horses in the world.

Iceland has the most important natural hot spring in the world (producing water at 245 litres per second).

Hey! Didn't I see you in that awful pun on page 202?

Over 70 per cent of South Koreans are connected to the internet. That's more than in any other country.

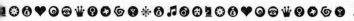
Latvia has the biggest proportion of women to men in the world – 54 per cent to 46 per cent men.

Canada has the longest coastline but more than half of it is accounted for by its many offshore islands.

Finland has more islands than any other country: 179,584.

Sudan has the highest number of border countries in Africa (nine countries).

Denmark is the world's top calorie-consuming country, with its citizens each consuming an average of 3,808 calories per day. The Americans come second, with 3,700 a day, and the world average is 2,745. Maybe that's why the people of Denmark are officially the happiest people on earth!

The border between North and South Korea is considered the most heavily fortified border in the world.

Animal adjectives

You probably know that a cat (and all things to do with a cat) is described as 'feline' and a dog as 'canine'. Here's how other creatures can be described.

Alligator – eusuchian
Ant – formicine
Ass – asinine
Badger – musteline
Bat – pteropine
Bee – apiarian
Calf – vituline
Camel – cameline
Chicken – galline
Crab – cancrine
Deer – cervine
Dolphin – delphine
Dormouse – myoxine
Elk – cervine
Flea – pulicine
Fox – vulpine
Frog – ranine

Giraffe – giraffine
Goat – caprine
Hamster – cricetine
Hippopotamus – hippopotamine
Human – hominine
Hyena – hyenine
Kangaroo – macropodine
Leopard – pardine
Lobster – homarine
Mole – talpine
Mouse – murine
Ox – bovine
Rat – murine
Reindeer – rangiferine
Rhinoceros – ceratorhine
Snake – ophidian
Squirrel – sciurine
Stag – cervine
Tiger – tigrine
Tortoise – chelonian
Wasp – vespine
Wombat – phascolomian
Worm – vermian
Zebra – zebrine

Sports and their specific superstitions

ANGLING

Spitting on your bait before casting your rod to make fish bite.

Not changing rods while fishing.

Throwing back your first catch for good luck.

Not telling anyone how many fish you've caught until you've finished (or, supposedly, you won't catch another).

BASEBALL

Spitting into the hand before picking up the bat.

Not stepping on the baselines while running off and on the field between innings.

Not lending a bat to another player.

Sticking some chewing-gum on a player's hat.

Making sure that a dog doesn't walk across the diamond before the first pitch.

BASKETBALL

Bouncing the ball before taking a foul shot.

The last person to shoot a basket during the warm-up will have a good game.

Wiping the soles of your sneakers for good luck.

CRICKET

Putting on kit in a certain order.

Hopping on one leg when the score is 111 (222, 333, etc.) if you're British.

FOOTBALL

Putting on the left boot before the right.

Not shaving during a winning run.

Not talking before a match.

GOLF

Starting with only odd-numbered clubs.

Not using a ball with a number higher than four.

Carrying coins in your pockets.

ICE HOCKEY

Not shouting 'shutout' in the locker room before the game.

Not allowing hockey sticks to be crossed.

Tapping the goalkeeper on his shin pads before a game.

TENNIS

Not holding more than two balls at a time when serving.

Avoiding wearing the colour yellow.

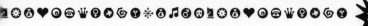

TEN-PIN BOWLING

Carrying charms.

Wearing the same clothes to continue a winning streak.

Putting the number 300, the sport's perfect score, on your licence plate.

Lasts

'Oh, Aunt Em, there's no place like home!' is the last line of the film *The Wizard of Oz*.

The England cricketer Andy Sandham played his last Test match in 1930 – during which he scored Test cricket's very first triple century (325).

Pitcairn Island is the last British territory in the Pacific.

King Manuel II, Portugal's last king, was deposed in 1910 and lived in exile in Twickenham, England.

The last time central London was flooded was in 1928, when the Thames burst its banks.

From birth to adolescence, selected bones in the human body fuse together. The last bone to fuse is the collarbone, and this occurs between the ages of 18 and 25.

In 1984 Liechtenstein became the last country in Europe to grant women the right to vote – and that was only after a referendum.

The Battle of Palmito Ranch (1865) was the last battle of the American Civil War. The battle was won by the Confederate (southern) forces, who actually lost the war.

In 1927 Alfred Bower became the last amateur player to captain the England football team.

Mitchell Symons
HOW TO AVOID A WOMBAT'S BUM*
And other fascinating facts!

* Don't chase it! Wombats can run up to 25 miles per hour and stop dead in half a stride. They kill their predators this way – the predator runs into the wombat's bum-bone and smashes its face.

Amaze and intrigue your friends and family with more fantastic facts and figures:

- most dinosaurs were no bigger than chickens

- Everton was the first British football club to introduce a stripe down the side of players' shorts

- A snail has about 25,000 teeth

- No piece of paper can be folded in half more than seven times

Just opening this book will have you hooked for hours!

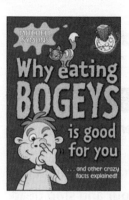

Mitchell Symons
WHY EATING BOGEYS IS GOOD FOR YOU
And other crazy facts explained!

Ever wondered . . .

- Why we have tonsils?
- Is there any cream in cream crackers?
- What's the best way to cure hiccups?
- And if kangaroos keep their babies in their pouches, what happens to all the poo?

Mitchell Symons answers all these wacky questions and plenty more in a wonderfully addictive book that will have you hooked for hours!

(And eating bogeys is good for you . . . but only your own!)

Selected for the Booktrust Booked Up! Initiative in 2008.

Mitchell Symons
HOW MUCH POO DOES AN ELEPHANT DO?*

. . . and further fascinating facts!

* An elephant produces an eye-wateringly pongy 20 kilograms of dung a day!

Let Mitchell Symons be your guide into the weird and wonderful world of trivia.

- Camels are born without humps
- Walt Disney, creator of Mickey Mouse, was scared of mice
- Only 30% of humans can flare their nostrils
- A group of twelve or more cows is called a flink

Mitchell Symons

WHY YOU NEED A PASSPORT WHEN YOU'RE GOING TO PUKE*

... and more crazy-but-true facts!

*Puke is the name of a town in Albania. Would YOU like to holiday there . . . ?

Did you know . . .

- **Square watermelons are sold in Japan**

- **There is a River Piddle in Dorset**

- **American use enough toilet paper daily to wrap around the world nine times**

Mitchell Symons goes global – join him on his fun fact-finding world tour!

Mitchell Symons

DON'T WIPE YOUR BUM WITH A HEDGEHOG

Top tips from the marvellous mind of Mitchell Symons.

- Why buy shampoo when real poo is free?

- **Never put both your feet in your mouth as you won't have a leg to stand on.**

- You can't trust a dog to watch your food.

- **And if getting even doesn't work, just get odd!**

Mitchell Symons knows the answers . . . and now you will too!